Embracing Erotic Wholeness

Embracing Erotic Wholeness:

From Shame to Curiosity

Esther M. Hooley, Ph.D.

Kardia Writing and Publishing

kardia
WRITING & PUBLISHING

ISBN: 979-8-9904713-1-3

For Miracle and Ja'vian.

May you grow up celebrating a love for yourself and a love for God.

Content Warning

This text contains some narrative that might be difficult to read including sexual assault. No graphic material is used, but we are impacted by stories. Feel free to skip over sections that you find distressing.

Table of Contents

Introduction

Unbinding

I have suffered the most in life when I was unable to locate my spirit or myself within my being. When I look at where things started to become especially painful, I think of it on a spiritual and sexual level. The pain that coils in my body began when I learned that my body was nothing but a receptacle. When my sexuality was warped and twisted by my perpetrators just as much as it was by purity culture.

The culture I was raised in was harmful. It taught me to hate myself, to think that I was worthless, to fear and expect punishment, to believe that everyone would always know more than me. It contributed to the theft of my ability to find emotional connection in sexuality. It displaced my ability to find the erotic within myself. It made sex the perpetual problem in my closest relationship. My culture contributed to the belief that I am obligated to have sex and that I am the master of the wellbeing of my partner as long as I am giving my body away. I am enraged that I have been used, or let myself be used, or wanted to be used and that I allowed myself to be, or become, just a body and not a being. I have and will likely continue to grieve that I often feel so far away from God. I want a way back to myself and a way back to my Creator. I am so tired of covering the parts of myself where there is pain and confusion only to mean I live disconnected.

I know that the writing rules state that "to engage a reader you have to tell a story." In some ways, that sentiment stopped me from writing this book for several years. I felt shame and took the path that, as a psychologist, I must keep my story hidden from others – keep the boundaries, be a blank slate. That reasoning was just my form of defense to stop myself from being vulnerable. I told myself, *"No one wants your story, Esther."* The thing is, I *know* that part of healing is telling your story. Not for others, but for yourself. It is healing that I am seeking by writing this book, and I hope it is healing that you find from reading it.

So here I am – inviting you in with a story....

There are so many parts of my childhood that I loved. Being outside, playing in the creek, watching the lightning bugs light up the side of the mountain I lived next to, playing flashlight tag while watching all the bats come out to fly for the night. There are so many beautiful images I hold of being happy and feeling safe, and of course, because we are human, there are some painful memories too.

In my early childhood, I lived in a small town in West Virginia. I grew up in a large family that I loved and love dearly. There was myself, my four siblings, and my mom and dad. My mom patiently (I don't know how she did it) homeschooled all five of us kids and our family attended church "every time the doors were open." We went to a small Baptist church or, more specifically, a "fundamental, independent, Bible" Baptist church. As you may be able to tell, it was conservative in nature. My family was shaped by its connection to the conservative faith of this church and its congregation. There is a fuzziness to my recall about this religion, but what I do know is that the values, rules, and messages within my home were shaped by the interpretations of this conservative faith.

Maybe as an adult I could have sifted through it all and made sense of it, but as a child, it felt scary. Things seemed clearly either/or: in or out, right or wrong, saved or damned. The message I heard told me that I was either good or bad, but mostly bad, and that's why I was a "sinner" and why Jesus had to die, something for which I was often told to be grateful. There was always a right or wrong, and if I chose wrong, it meant I was wrong and I was punished. I felt fearful for much of my childhood, and this is where the roots of shame begin to squeeze my heart and paralyze me. So, I was baptized twice, as I was afraid the first baptism didn't take. I spent many nights praying for salvation in terror that I would die in my sleep and end up in hell.

I grew up with this faith during some very important moments of time. Time when my brain was taking information in, assimilating, or accommodating, and beginning to understand the world through the lens of these religious messages. My brain was creating neural pathways. My attachment bonds and wounds were being created. All these parts of me were being formed while feelings of fear and shame were roaming in my body and taking root.

As I was growing up, the idea of purity and sex came into focus. Typically, it was at church camp, or from hearing my parent's rules about courtship and chaperones, or from someone teaching at a pulpit. Outside of my family, the messages about purity came from middle-aged white men who appeared very concerned about the sexuality of a young teenage girl. When I look back, it is baffling that we were all okay with this. Sex was talked about like it was the ultimate sin. Murder, stealing and adultery – these were terrible sins, yes, but sex – the fiery flames of hell are being stoked as we speak.

During these young years, I made covenants with God (at the suggestion of said middle-aged men) that my purity would remain intact until after I was married. I learned that to break this covenant and no longer be a virgin would mean I would have to beg Jesus to restore my purity and to pray that some man, someday, would still find me worthy of marriage or love. I was petrified. By this time, I was questioning whether I was loved in my family and wondered if something was wrong with me. The stakes felt so high. Not only was I already convinced I was bad and believed Jesus saw me as bad, but now, there was something even more terrifying. If I could not keep my purity for my future husband, then he and others would know that I really was all bad. There would be no chance for me to prove myself "good" and to have someone love me. Since I really did want to be loved, I made an effort to get my first boyfriend. I met him when I turned sixteen, and it was shortly after my 16th birthday that I was sexually assaulted.

It's taken me a long time to be able to name that experience as sexual assault. To not hear the echo of religious teachings about how I had done something very wrong by engaging in a sexual act. The unraveling started there. It's hard to describe the feelings that occur after an unwanted sexual experience. It's confusing. There are gaps in memory. The body no longer feels like it belongs to you, and there is a soul-crushing shame that can take root in the soul. After this violation occurred (almost immediately), all the sermons, religious messages, traumatizing demonstrations about what it means about a woman if she is not a virgin when she marries seemed to bloom within me. My greatest fears seemed to be coming true.

I hated myself. I hated God. And, just like that, I was back to childhood – I had done something wrong, the worst thing I could do. So, I believed that God couldn't stand me. I believed God was ashamed of me and rejected me. So, I rejected myself. I had no value. No one would ever love me. God would never love me. It was over. I had committed the ultimate sin. Now, I'm going to pause here because I want to be very clear that I believe that being sexually assaulted is NOT "committing" anything. Assault and violence is something *done to you*. It was not and will never be your fault that you or me were assaulted. This was just how my young brain and the accompanying trauma tried to make sense of things.

I didn't know what to do except to blame myself. The shame was suffocating. What I was taught through my religion felt true. I was bad. I was wrong. I could never be good again. That's a lot for a kid to feel, and I wanted very much to not feel anything. As is often true for those who have experienced an unwanted sexual experience, I used some pretty damaging coping mechanisms as I worked to stop feeling, and I ended up in situations that led to several more unwanted sexual experiences. I didn't learn until I was in my graduate training that putting oneself in dangerous situations often occurs as a result of having experienced an unwanted sexual encounter. I was just trying my best to go numb. If I couldn't feel anything, then maybe I wouldn't have to feel shame.

The stance I took towards God was one of fear. When I look back now, the picture that comes to mind is that of Eve hiding in the garden of Eden, squeezing her eyes shut, holding her breath, waiting to hear her fate. I felt I deserved banishment just like her, and I banished myself – cutting myself off from my body, my wants, and the belief that I could be enough. I tried in so many ways to understand why, to find reasons that justified my experiences. There had to be something!

I could have gone to therapy when I became an adult, but I didn't. I told myself I didn't need therapy. Ironically, but not surprisingly, I became a therapist instead. I was searching for answers and healing, but at the same time, I continued to feel like I didn't deserve to understand. Then, I decided to become a Ph.D. student – *maybe this would be the thing*. I was still searching. So, I wrote a dissertation to try to find something – maybe it was because I didn't learn about sex the "right" way, maybe it's because I had intergenerational wiring that would set me up to be traumatized. Maybe this. Maybe that. If I could just figure it out, then maybe I could be good again. The truth is, there was no why, and still, that truth is one I work to accept every day.

So, here I am now – an adult, a psychologist, someone who has gone to therapy and treats trauma in therapy, someone who devotes time to engage in sexual restoration in relationships and who works to help people find their own sexual healing. But I still feel so much for that little girl afraid of being rejected, and I feel for the teenager who was afraid of being banished by God. I also feel for the adult Me who still gets triggered and scared.

Purity culture and conservative religion are the parents to my shame, and I no longer want to be part of that family. This has been and will be my journey. I don't get it right some days, and shame still lives in my body, but I have been able to do some work around rejecting ideas about purity determining my worth. I've had to work on beliefs such as "sex separates us from God" and that "I have to work to be good enough" because of what was done to me without my consent. Some days I feel more healed than others, and I'm alright with that. The hope is that while I write this book, I continue to find space to breathe and to connect with my body and story and that you are able to experience this with me.

I know that there is a magnitude of material coming out about purity culture, and I feel so encouraged about this. It says to me that people are doing their own work and offering what they know to each other in the name of healing and hope, and I know that purity culture hasn't really left us yet. We see it showing up in our politics (Roe v. Wade) and even in our homogenous churches (white is seen as pure, and we are still impacted by racist ideas about people's bodies). My hope is that this book adds to what we know and helps you as you continue to encounter purity culture in your community, your sexuality, and in the church.

What you will find in the chapters ahead is a brief introduction to purity culture and the impact it has on the mind, body, and spirit. You will explore shame and move towards the parts of you that sit in pain. We will look at how shame feels in your soul and in your body and how it is the ultimate disconnector. Then, we will get curious about reconnection and embodiment. Once we are feeling settled (enough) we will dig into sex topics that are typically seen as either/or...or avoided altogether. I hope that we can begin to see how sexuality is something that can be let out and made a part of our lives, which may also bring us closer not only to ourselves but to our God.

Chapter One

The Purity Paradox

Hearing the words "purity culture" creates a strong reaction in me. I often feel tenderness, knowing that what is likely to come after those words is someone's story of pain, confusion, and shame. In fact, in all my years as a therapist, a pleasant story has never followed those two words. Beyond sadness, there is a great rage that fills my body. It is a sacred rage. It is a rage of remembrance, and what it remembers is that many have silenced an important part of who they were made to be because of a religion that said sexuality could be done "right or wrong" in the eyes of a God that created sexuality to be a part of each person to varying degrees. It is a rage that remembers all the ways people have abandoned their own bodies because of the messages they were given while their young minds were being formed, and are still ringing in their ears to this day. This rage lingers in our collective memory of purity culture, and it is perhaps our deepest collective shame.

A Short History

Purity culture began in the 1990s, coming out of the Evangelical Protestant Christian world, and it took off from there. Purity culture refers to an allegedly "biblical" view of sexuality, specifically sexual purity. It does this by vilifying secular or "traditional" aspects of sexuality expressed in relationships. This culture holds that virginity should be "protected" and "saved" until marriage occurs between two (male and female), monogamous, heterosexual, cisgendered people. Purity culture essentially repackaged sexual judiciousness as a measure of a person's worth, how dedicated they were to faith and to God, and to purity in general. The movement was created with a purpose. It was the evangelical response to the "sin" that came along with free-love, pro-choice and contraceptive activism, the women's liberation movement, and the AIDS epidemic (Edger, pp.164-165, 2012).

The Evangelical community was rife with literature to increase the position of abstinence only. Some familiar ones include *I Kissed Dating Goodbye, Every Young Man's Battle, Every Young Woman's Battle, Love and Respect,* and *The Christian Charm Course/Curriculum.* These works painted a picture of how every man and woman should experience and explore sexuality, which was to say "don't." These books often set unrealistic standards because they actually go against basic human drives. These drives – such as sex, arousal, longing, curiosity, and attraction – are basic in humans, and we were told they must be subdued, controlled, and repented of. In fact, if a person could not change these human reactions, then they were looked down upon or even viewed as harlots, which is a Bible word for slut (I'm using it because women were often seen in a more negative light than men when it came to sexuality and mostly still are).

Beyond books and youth groups, there were church camps, "lock-ins" (where youth groups are "locked-in" to a church for the night), conferences, Christian magazines and parental teachings that marketed this message. It may be that purity and abstinence were meant to be something wonderful, but in reality, the values, themes, and teachings often targeted females more than males, which some research suggests led to the internalization of shame that then impacted the relationship females had with their own sexuality (Wind, 2017).

Abstinence Only Sex Education

Another significant outcome of the purity movement was the shift in sex education that occurred. As purity culture was gaining steam, the movement proposed an abstinence only model. In fact, the Reagan administration was the first to provide funding for abstinence only sex education (Klein, 2018). That is, sex education was framed as promoting no sex until marriage as the main form of STI/STD and pregnancy prevention. While these teachings began in religious institutions, public policy also came into effect ensuring that public schools also taught abstinence only curriculum (Boyer, 2020).

While we would like to think "that was the 90s," it is worth noting that the SIECUS (Sex Ed for Social Change) report of 2022 showed that 30 states are currently required to emphasize the importance of abstinence only within sex education. This is a profound revelation of the long lasting hold the purity movement continues to have, even on public policy. Beyond public policy and American society, purity culture continues to have a lasting effect on church culture as well.

Often, teachings about purity culture were accompanied by demonstrations of how a person who no longer is a virgin is seen by others and their future partner. For example, there are stories of youth groups where teens would line up, and the youth group leader would hold up one cup representing virginity or a virgin. The cup was passed around, and each teen would be asked to spit into the cup until the last person in line was left with the spit-filled cup. An object "lesson" was then given about how a person who has sexual experiences before marriage is like a cup filled with spit. The last person holding the cup represented the partner who waited until marriage to have sex, now left with a used and "disgusting" partner.

Who would want such a defiled thing? The cup is disgusting. Every teenager in the room would be terrified – would they be rejected, unwanted, disgusting to a future partner if they were not "pure?" These types of "lessons" were taught from pulpits to homes, and the message was clear. Any sexual activity a female engaged in turned her into a pre-licked lollipop, a used tissue, an unwrapped gift, or a rose without petals. In addition, when any of these comparisons were identified, it was presented as how women were perceived on their wedding night – used, worn-out, useless objects (Klein, 2018).

The Scripts We Were Given

Purity culture also created scripts around gender and sexuality through the lens of heteronormativity and gender as binary. These scripts became guidelines related to appropriate ways that sexual desires, behaviors (when, where, why, with whom, and how), sexuality, and gender should be expressed. Purity promotes the idea of a stereotype-based script of gender. One example is to look at how an inherent part of purity culture is to place heteronormative assumptions about sexuality and gender onto others resulting in perpetuating homophobia through heterosexist values and practices that are seen as the only ones to be emulated or practiced (Miller, 2017).

Men were told to be "masculine" – tough, strong, non-emotional, leaders at work, at home, at church. What a disservice that men were, in large part, encouraged to separate themselves from emotions, which is the thing that would bring about the truest connection with a partner. Not only was there a "be tough" mentality, but in some ways, purity culture told the world that men were beasts. Wild, untamed, sex-crazed mammals who lusted with their hearts and eyes. It was expected that males should have a voracious sexual appetite and have sexuality that could not be contained. To resist this belief was to reject what was seen as "natural" – a part of the male nature – to be unpredictable and wield spontaneous desire, arousal, lust, or an overall hypersexual drive. In this framing of sexuality, purity culture offered us a highly distorted view of both men and women. If women are hypersexualized objects of desire and reception, then men are hypersexed objects of arousal mindlessly pursuing receptacles for their appetite. Both are objectified. Both are dehumanized.

In line with this more beastly, or "caveman," image of men, purity culture purported that men are the only ones who have rights to pursue someone for a romantic relationship. This pressure before marriage – being the one to always be rejected or turned down – carries into marriage and has a highly detrimental "one-way" effect on the relationship. The script men were given was that they should pursue and have sex when they want. Once married, sex will be never ending, and your wife will always want sex with you. In fact, after you say, "I do," the picture that is painted is that a new wife will be just as sex crazed as you are and his and her level of arousal will be stable over time. This is an entirely one-way view of sexuality within a relationship, and paradoxically, it also sets the man up to be highly vulnerable.

I'm picturing a young, potentially sexually inexperienced male who has not been provided comprehensive sex education, believing that his job is to pursue a woman for sexual pleasure. His script tells him that he must always pursue, always risk, and this is framed as sexual prowess and dominance. But what vulnerability this demands! And, what if it doesn't "work" like he has been told it will? What if there is pain in intercourse, or fear, low desire, or erectile inconsistency? This, to me, is one of the saddest parts of purity culture. A man begins his life with a female partner and the sex isn't working like they were told it would. Picture a person who is constantly making themselves vulnerable to sexually connect with a spouse who does not want the same things. Over time, a person could begin to doubt he is loved, attractive, desired by his spouse, and his confidence is greatly impacted. Who does he turn to? He has been told not to feel, to be strong, and to exercise his sexual rights. What a lonely place to be.

There were also stereo-typed expectations for females in purity culture. Women were to be passive yet emotional, soft, feminine, focused on the role of wife/mother, and to be hospitable. Beyond this, there was a narrative that women were to live a life preparing to tend to husband and home. What purity culture did was to add another layer to these expectations. Not only were all people expected to hold a western view of gender, but in a religious context, women were given a script that told them to focus on romanticism, submissiveness, devotedness to one partner (monogamy), and, also, to be the "guard" against the sexual advances of males. Purity culture puts the responsibility of male sexuality into the hands of women. Women were told it was their job to monitor and control their own lust, as well as the lust that men would express. "It's women and girls' responsibility to dress right, to act right, to talk right, to do everything just right to ensure non-sexuality for all people" (Klein, 2018; in an interview with National Public Radio).

Once marriage occurs, women are still holding the belief that it is their job to manage their spouses' sexuality, and this often comes in the form of feeling obligated to have sex whenever their partner propositions them for sex. *Research of an Evangelical View of Sex* by Gregoire et al. (2021) makes multiple references to texts identifying the main message toward women as "his need for sex is bigger than your (female's) need for anything else." In a way, this culture groomed women to neglect their own physical and emotional experiences during sex, so that their husband's sexuality became the priority. I have heard the sorrow and seen the tears of women who were told to see sex as a beautiful and romantic part of a relationship but are unable to connect their minds to their bodies during sex.

Beyond the heteronormative expectation that all women will be married to men and the objectification that their bodies and sexuality no longer belong to them (but to their husbands), there is an expectation that the night of a woman's wedding she will be competent enough to satisfy her husband sexually despite a lifetime of sexual anorexia, guilt, and shame (Klein, 2018; Sellers, 2017). At this point, the reality usurps the fantasy, and the woman is faced with deep shame and many questions, such as "Am I withholding if I say no? If I say no, am I truly a Christian wife? Is something wrong with me for not wanting this like I thought I would?" The end result? Men feeling rejected, women feeling disconnected. What a set-up for marriage to be rife with conflict, for both partners to build resentment towards one another when reality does not reflect the fantasy.

When we look at the impact of purity and abstinence only teachings, we begin to see the full picture of harm that occurs. The tenets of purity teaching led to many women feeling shame and insecurity about their sexuality, women feeling as if it is their job to be responsible for the sexuality of men, and people being disconnected from their own bodies as they try to resist a natural and instinctive part of humanity. Beyond this, lack of comprehensive sex education led to benightedness regarding sex and deep shame when married. Finally, being "free" to engage in sex once married did not measure up to the unrealistic standards they were taught not only to believe in but that these standards were given by God.

The pressures and stereotypes that purity culture created for men and women are tragic. However, Emmerink et al. (2016) found that women's mental, emotional, and sexual health are more significantly impacted by these stereotypes. Their study found a higher risk for negative sexual and mental health distress among females who affirmed traditional gender roles.

Other research corroborated these findings in a study that connected gender inequality and female wellbeing, affirming the interplay of psychological, social, and biological factors of women's health (Mccool-Myers et al., 2018). Furthermore, Nagowski (2015) identified how the stereotype that men's sexual needs are innate, while a women's needs are practically nonexistent, lead to women mistrusting their minds and bodies in every sexual situation. Constant mistrust can lead to feelings of being "wrong" or "guilty" for women on the spectrum of sexual desire or no desire because most have been taught not to want sex while, at the same time, feeling responsible for meeting the "needs" of men.

Portions of what is mentioned above relates to sexual scripts. Sexual scripts are the approved norms regarding sexuality that a person learns, embraces, and endorses through a process of socialization (Simon and Gagnon, 1986). One could say that the script becomes what a person considers "normal" or "abnormal" when it comes to sex and sexuality. The theory behind sexual scripts says that sexual scripts are embedded in a cultural context where cultural norms create the guidelines for what is appropriate (in terms of behaviors, feelings, thoughts) for men and women regarding sexual experiences. Cultural factors that could contribute to the creation of a sexual script include family messages or communication about sex, available sex education, religious messaging, trauma (individual or systemic), and media.

The scripts then become models that individuals use to interpret and respond to sexual situations (Rose and Frieze, 1993). It is usually expected that people look to these scripts when judging their sexual experience and when engaging in sexual experiences (Stephens and Eaton, 2014). Sexuality is learned from what cultural messages are available to set guidelines regarding sexual behaviors and activities, whether shame, stereotypes, or falsehoods are involved in the creation of these messages.

I want to be forthcoming and say that I truly don't know if every person who experienced purity culture and abstinence only teachings had experiences like the ones mentioned in this chapter. That is not really the claim I am making here. What I do know is that many individuals, regardless of gender, have a sexual script formed by the Evangelical teachings of purity.

Rape and Objectification

As the title of this section indicates, rape and assault will be mentioned in the following paragraphs. It is not often expected that purity culture has connections to rape or objectification; however, recent research makes a compelling case for this connection. Nagowski (2015), for example, stated that moral messaging regarding female sexuality often reduces women to their sexual organs, identifying that, for women, "your virginity is your most valuable asset." I am aware that it was not the intent of purity culture to tell women "You are to be used," but unfortunately, this is what many women heard.

This usage takes a person out of their own body, silences the voices of women, and offers one the realization that they are being viewed only as a container for pleasure or violence. Often, when a body is used for someone else against personal wishes, coping can come in the form of dissociation or spectatoring, which is another barrier to pleasure and connection as the body and mind disconnect. It is worth noting that recent research (Owens et al., 2020) demonstrates that endorsement of purity culture is related to increased endorsement of rape myths while also increasing the likelihood of labeling both marital and acquaintance rape as consensual sex.

Some recent research was able to find that Christian dating books, which promoted sexual abstinence, also promoted rape culture (Klement and Sagarin, 2016). The 2016 study found three themes related to rape culture that were prominent in Christian dating books (for adults and adolescents). The first theme was "Women are responsible for the sexual violence that men perpetrate." You may be thinking that you didn't explicitly read this in Christian books but messaging around men being powerless to fight their sexual urges, men who are visual and become aroused even by fully clothed or "modest" women, is a part of purity messaging. These messages align with the common rape myth that rape is a natural consequence of an over-active and uncontrollable male sex-drive. In the Christian book, *Dateable: Are you? Are they?* Lookadoo and DiMarco (2003) inform readers that girls are "asking for it" when dressed a particular way. Ethridge and Arterburn (2004) also tell of how flirting and dressing in a provocative manner will lead to a woman being taken advantage of. In *I Kissed Dating Goodbye,*

Harris (1997, p.50) uses an example about a woman who is unable to save her virginity because she is "placing herself in compromising situations." These messages may not be overt to the eyes of young readers, but they do imply that women are responsible if rape or assault occurs.

The second theme that showed up in Klement and Sagarin's 2016 study was "Women should expect and accept sexual violence as a normal part of life." In *Every Young Woman's Battle: Guarding Your Mind, Heart, and Body in a Sex-Saturated World* (Ethridge and Arterburn, 2004, p. 98), the authors use an anecdotal story to make their point by focusing on the negative consequences that women brought on themselves, rather than focusing on the perpetrator or how these girls said "no." Their main message becomes, as girls flirt with boys (particularly older boys) a natural consequence is to be objectified and sexualized. Other authors (Lookadoo and DiMarco, 2003) present the reader with the idea that men will always try to pressure a woman to go further sexually than she wants, highlighting that women should expect men will "pressure" or coerce females into sex.

The final theme of the 2016 study was "Women who are not submissive should be derogated." This theme of rape culture demonstrates how a woman should be treated if she does not follow the "rules." In some works (Driscoll and Driscoll, 2012; Ethridge and Arterburn, 2004; Lookadoo and DiMarco, 2003), the acceptable woman is characterized by being abstinent and submissive. The "other" type of woman is manipulative, seeks to sexually tempt men, or only wants sex because it is pleasurable. These types of tropes spell out hostile sexism. Additionally, it is worth noting that more recent research show that purity culture and rape culture are found to be linked both cognitively and causally (Klement, Sagarin, and Skowronski, 2022).

Objectification theory posits that the incessant sexual objectification experienced by women directly correlates to women's mental health (Fredrickson and Roberts,1997). These researchers believed that the impact of this objectification led to an increased risk of "eating disorders, sexual dysfunction, anxiety, and depression" as they began to understand their bodies externally by what's known as "self-objectification" (Koval et al., 2019). Objectification theory also suggests that the cultural condition of objectification functions to socialize females to, at some level, begin to treat themselves as objects that are to be looked at and evaluated (Fredrickson and Roberts,1997).

Objectification can be thought of as a third-person view of self that leads to a constant monitoring of appearance (a self-surveillance), the result of which is often shame and anxiety. Monitoring leads to comparison and often a feeling of "less than" or "not enough." When these emotions begin to build, women then disconnect from their internal experiences, and this results in a decreasing ability to be present in the moment, which can be correlated to decreased sexual satisfaction (Emmerink, et al., 2016). Surprisingly, another study (Koval et al., 2019) found that women can experience emotions such as anger, shame, guilt, and embarrassment even if sexual objectification is witnessed and not specifically directed towards them. This significant insight tells us that the witnessing of sexual objectification of others also results in internal self-objectification.

As mentioned above, objectification theory posits that female sexual experiences are impacted by self-conscious body-monitoring and body-based shame and anxiety, taking attention away from the internal experience and focusing on external presentation (Fredrickson and Robert, 1997). If a person is constantly focused on her body, then the mental energy that could have gone into arousal and desire is hijacked. What this can result in is something known as "spectatoring" during sexual experiences. Spectatoring, coined by Masters and Johnson (1970), is where attention is on the body versus in the body, which makes arousal and orgasm more difficult. The worst consequence of objectification, however, results in sexual abuse, assault, or harassment. Clearly, these experiences impact women's enjoyment of sex. Research shows that those who encounter such dehumanizing forms of objectification commonly experience a reduction of sexual enjoyment (Gordon & Riger, 1989). Some older research further indicates that satisfaction with sex can remain lower than it previously was for up to seven years following sexual trauma (Feldman-Summers, Gordon, & Maegher, 1979).

I recently learned of a story in which two men were talking about sexuality, particularly masturbation, and one person noted that they couldn't wait to get married because then they would not be committing the "sin" of viewing pornography and masturbating. While I don't have the full context of this conversation, one could infer that the implication was that once married, a partner (in this case female) will be able to satisfy all sexual needs of this man. While I have empathy for the messages this man received that led him to these conclusions, I also notice how these messages will impact his partner and not just him. At some point, this man, and likely many others, were told that there would be no need for self-pleasure because their virgin wife will take care of all their sexual needs. It is this assumption that is a result of the foundational script telling a man that a woman's body can be used in any way that will fulfill his sexual desires. Again, although I don't think this was the intent of purity culture, it is definitely a part of it. This script also implies that men can expect to have complete and immediate access to the body of their wife, which results in a secondary (and perhaps more insidious) consequence – the objectification and dehumanization of a spouse.

While religious culture often abhors pornography (a space where women are often objectified), there appears to be no hesitation in promoting the objectification of a spouse. Finding sexual pleasure in a spouse is often framed as "she will give her body to you", but often, for women who have been a part of purity culture – with its lack of education, heightening of female voices, and suppression of connection with body – the "giving" can feel like a taking. Emily Nagoski (2015) identifies the inherent risks in promoting a position that women are "things" to be used to alleviate men's "needs." Other authors (Gregoire et al., 2021) acknowledge how many women have just become a bodily repository for husbands to orgasm into in an effort to keep themselves from being tempted to relieve their profound lust in other ways.

Racial Considerations

It is important to identify that most of purity culture rhetoric, conversation, and outcries are made by or focused solely on the white woman's experience. Tragically, the experiences of white women are taken as a universal understanding for all women. To take such a narrow focus, however, leads to the exclusion of the voices and stories of women of color. The results of which have been devastating as these happenings continue a pattern of gendered racism that is also currently embedded within the evangelical faith.

Natarajan and colleagues (2022) note that absent from the purity culture conversation are the ways in which purity culture centers whiteness by claiming the ideal embodiment of sexual purity as only showing up in attractive white females thereby ignoring women who identify as Black, Asian, Latina, Indigenous, or Multiracial. The centering of the white, hetero, cis, able-bodied thin narrative leads to the implication that women of color are "innately impure" (Anderson, 2015). White body supremacy shows up in physical form by elevating the white body as the standard that all other persons are measured against (Menakem, 2017). There has often been the association between whiteness and purity, meaning that women of color, more specifically Black and Indigenous women, are often not included in the idea of sexual purity. The racial stereotypes that depict women of color as hypersexual enhance this discussion of racial diversity from purity tenets.

Racial purity rhetoric can be traced back to sexual violence perpetuated by white men against enslaved women and girls during chattel slavery. These actions illuminate how historical atrocities contributed to the view of white women as "ideal." The bodies of Black women and girls were assumed to be expendable and rape-able while white women's bodies were to be cared for with paramount respect (Feinstein, 2016). Others have postulated that rape culture is a result of white heteropatriarchy and is used to sustain white male control over any group that threatens this control (Kessel, 2022). The unsettling and profound conclusion to be highlighted here is that whiteness and white supremacy are indissolubly linked to both purity culture and rape culture.

Because of the universal belief that these enslaved Black bodies were disposable, they were often used to be assaulted by white slave owners, which created a narrative of the "hypersexualized" Black woman. These falsehoods regarding the hypersexuality of Black and Brown women are used historically to justify the sexual violence white male slave owners would inflict on the enslaved. The falsely constructed images of Black women (i.e. Mammies and Jezebels) created by a society designed to oppress, contributed to and perpetuated stereotypes that paint Black women as hypersexual, deserving of punishment and pity, and have hypersexualized young Black girls (Cooper, 2018). There is a notable privilege that white women have when we acknowledge the gendered, racist, sexualization that black women experience in ways that white women do not experience. Gendered racism (oppression that is present due to race and gender), similar to the constructs created both within the church and in slavery, helped to give birth to the belief that Black women are the antithesis of the ideal pure women, which has subsequently impacted "the need for Blacks to prove their sexual purity and Christ-like moral agency" (Day, p. 25, 2018).

Purity culture and anti-Asian racism also intersect. In 2021, a gunman opened fire at three Atlanta-area spas killing eight people, six of which were Asian women. His motive was due to a "sex addiction" and a "temptation for him that he wanted to eliminate." Christine Hong, a professor at Columbia Theological Seminary, noted that this rationale shows a toxic recipe of Christian purity messages. She notes, "Sexual purity theologies are tied to white supremacy because Asian women have a transcontinental history of being hypersexualized and fetishized through Orientalism and militarism in Asian nations" (NBC News Interview, 2021). Hong continues by highlighting that you could be an aged grandmother whose role is to feed co-workers at an Asian-owned spa, and then, suddenly, you are viewed as a "sex worker" or a temptress for white men. As stated earlier in this chapter, purity culture focuses on abstaining from temptation but also that women can be objectified or seen as a sexual vessel. This messaging seemingly erases the personhood and identity of these murdered Asian women, and instead, it classifies them as temptations to be eliminated. By erasing the "temptation" the shooter felt afflicted by, he was able to maintain his own righteousness.

It is worth noting that before immigration policy change in 1965, many Korean women were brought to the United States as brides of American servicemen. Many or most of these women met their husbands as sex workers in Korea. Some Asian America scholars link the hypersexualization of Asian women in the States to the influx of sex work around military bases in Asia. However, K. Christine Pae (NBC News, 2021) notes that this hypersexualization dates to early European church beliefs in which anything associated with the physical body was seen as sinful, and historically, women and people of color were seen as being closer to the body. Pae noted, "Sexuality is still also associated with Christian imagination of sin, especially original sin" resulting in women of color being seen as especially sexual. Similar to the "Mammie/Jezebel" dichotomy, Asian women were often placed in a virgin/whore dichotomy perpetuated by the Christian church. This also played out on military bases where servicemen were there to protect "good women" – their wives, girlfriends, mothers – while using "sinful women" (Asian women) who were considered sexually available and rape-able (Pae in NBC News Interview, 2021). Sadly, this only serves to confirm how women were segregated into camps of "good" or "bad" likely based on ethnicity.

Research is lacking regarding the impact of purity culture on other specific ethnicities, possibly implying it is thought of as unnecessary, but also leaving a gap in the understanding of the full female experience regarding purity. The silence around female sexuality, for both women of color and white women, fails to acknowledge the feelings, thoughts, and desires that arise during a female's physical maturation. The final result is that intentionally sexually uneducated, female, evangelical youths are disempowered to exercise their own individual agency. Furthermore, the limited and pejorative language about sexuality that exists in the evangelical church negatively impacts the perception many females have of their bodies and desires, inducing trauma, shame, and isolation, while also impacting their relationship with their future sexual partners and, ultimately, with God.

Shame

I'll touch briefly on shame as we will be taking a deep dive in the next chapter. Shame is the reason I wanted to write this book – my own sexual shame that turned into whole-person shame and being the witness to others' shame in hours of psychotherapy. The damage that shame causes is catastrophic. Klein (p.14, 2018) states that "the purity message is not about sex. Rather, it is about us: who we are, who we are expected to be, and who it is said we will become if we fail to meet those expectations. This is the language of shame." Because shame involves the whole self, sexual shame is often related to an individual's concept of their bodies and therefore contributes to overall feelings of worthlessness and a sense of inadequacy.

When we determine something is worthless in our lives, what do we do with it? We toss it out! We say, "Not good enough," and we create distance between us and the worthless thing. When we cut ourselves off from our bodies, sexuality, pleasure, and the right to have desire, we are silencing fundamental parts of ourselves. This results in a reinforcement of the idea that there is something wrong with us, and who we are is transgressed to the core.

Get Curious

1. Reflect on your own sexual script. What influences shaped your script? Has it changed over time? Is the script aligned with you and your values right now?

2. What is your definition of shame? Recall a time you felt shame. What did you notice? What thoughts or emotions were present? How did your body respond?

3. When was the first time you became aware you had a body? When was the first time you recall others becoming aware of your body? How has objectification or self-objectification impacted your experience of yourself?

Chapter One References

Anderson D. (2015). *Damaged goods: New perspectives on Christian purity*. Jericho Books.

Boyer, J. (2020, March 04). New name, same harm: Rebranding of federal abstinence-only programs. Retrieved August 31, 2020, from https://www.guttmacher.org/gpr/2018/02/new-name-same-harm-rebranding-federal-abstinence-only-programs.

Cooper, B. C. (2018). *Eloquent rage: A black feminist discovers her superpower*. Martin's Press.

Driscoll, M. & Driscoll, G. (2012). *Real marriage: The truth about sex, friendship, and life together*. Thomas Nelson.

Edger, K. (2012). Evangelicalism, sexual morality, and sexual addiction: opposing views and continued conflicts. *Journal of Religious Health*, 51(1), 162-178. doi: 10.1007/s10943-010-9338-7. PMID: 20182916.

Emmerink, P. M. J., Van Den Eijnden, R.J. J. M., Vanwesenbeeck, I., & Ter Bogt, T. F. (2016). The relationship between endorsement of the sexual double standard and sexual cognitions and emotions. *Sex Roles*, 75(7), 363–376. doi: 10.1007/s11199-016-0616-z.

Ethridge, S. & Arterburn, S. (2004). *Every young woman's battle: Guarding your mind, heart, and body in a sex-saturated world*. WaterBrook & Multnomah.

Feinstein R. (2016). Intersectionality and the role of white women: An analysis of divorce petitions from slavery. *Journal of Historical Sociology*, 30(3), 545–560. doi: 10.1111/johs.12125.

Feldman-Summers, S., Gordon, P. E., & Maegher, J. R. (1979). The impact of rape on sexual satisfaction. *Journal of Abnormal Psychology*, 88, 101-105.

Fredrickson, B. L. & Roberts, T. A. (1997). Objectification theory: Toward understanding women's lived experiences and mental health risks. *Psychology of Women Quarterly*, 21(2), 173–206. doi: 10.1111/j.1471-6402.1997.tb00108.x.

Gregoire, S. W., Lindenbach, R. G., & Sawatsky, J. (2021). *The great sex rescue: The lies you've been taught and how to recover what god intended.* Baker Books.

Gordon, M. T. & Riger, S. (1989). *The female fear: The social cost of rape.* Free Press.

Harris, J. (1997). *I kissed dating goodbye.* Multnomah Books.

Klein, L. K. (2018). *Pure: Inside the religious movement that shamed a generation of young women and how we broke free.* Touchstone.

Klein, L. (2018, September 18). *Memorist: evangelical purity movement sees women's bodies as a threat.* [Radio Broadcast]. NPR https://www.npr.org/2018/09/18/648737143/memoirist-evangelical-purity-movement-sees-womens-bodies-as-a-threat.

Koval, P., Holland, E., Zyphur, M. J., Stratemeyer, M., Knight, J. M., Bailen, N. H., & Haslam, N. (2019). How does it feel to be treated like an object? Direct and indirect effects of exposure to sexual objectification on women's emotions in daily life. *Journal of Personality and Social Psychology*, 116(6), 885–898. doi: 10.1037/pspa0000161.

Klement, K. R., Sagarin, B. J., & Skowronski, J. J. (2022). The one ring model: rape culture beliefs are linked to purity culture beliefs. *Sexuality & Culture*, 26, 2070–2106. doi: 10.1007/s12119-022-09986-2.

Lyons, H., Giordano, P. C., Manning, W. D., & Longmore, M. A. (2011). Identity, peer relationships, and adolescent girls' sexual behavior: an exploration of the contemporary double standard. *Journal of Sex Research*, 48(5), 437–449. doi: 10.1080/00224499.2010.506679.

Masters, W. H. & Johnson, V. E. (1970). *Human sexual inadequacy.* Little Brown.

Miller J. (2017). Queering the virgin: evangelical world-making and the heterosexual crisis. *European Journal of American Studies*, 11(11–3), Article 11. doi: 10.4000/ejas.11818.

Natarajan, M., Wilkins-Yel, K. G., Sista, A., Anantharaman, A., & Seils, N. (2022). Decolonizing purity culture: gendered racism and white idealization in Evangelical Christianity. *Psychology of Women Quarterly*, 46(3), 316–336. doi: 10.1177/03616843221091116.

Rose, S. & Frieze, I. (1993). Young singles' contemporary dating scripts. *Sex Roles*, 28, 499–509. doi: 10.1007/BF00289677.

SEICUS. https://siecus.org/the-siecus-state-profiles-2022/.

Simon, W. & Gagnon, J. H. (1986) Sexual scripts: permanence and change. *Archives of Sexual Behaviour*, 15, 97–120. doi: 10.1007/BF01542219.

Stephens, D. & Eaton, A. (2014). The influence of masculinity scripts on heterosexual Hispanic college men's perceptions of female-initiated sexual coercion. *Psychology of Men & Masculinity*, 15, 387–396. doi: 10.1037/a0034639.

Wind, R. (2017, August 22). Abstinence-only-until-marriage programs are ineffective and harmful to young people, expert review confirms. Retrieved from https://www.guttmacher.org/news-release/2017/abstinence-only-until-marriage-programs-are-ineffective-and-harmful-young-people.

Chapter Two

Disentangling Sexuality and Shame

If distress is the effect of suffering, shame is the effect of indignity, transgression and of alienation. Though terror speaks to life and death and distress makes the world avail of tears, yet shame strikes deepest into the heart of man. Shame is felt as an inner torment, a sickness of the soul, the humiliated one feels himself naked, defeated, alienated, lacking in dignity and worth. (Tomkins as cited in Adamson & Clark, 1999, p. 23).

Does anyone else's mind go straight to Game of Thrones when you hear the word shame? That moment where Cersei Lannister is forced to walk naked through the streets of King's Landing as penance for her adultery. Interesting that the humiliation of the character was in part because all parts of her body were visible (inviting the viewer to see that nudity and shame are connected). Interestingly, one of the creators of the show noted that the walk of shame scene was made to mimic a scene from someone's nightmare. My thought is that Cersei was not ashamed because of adultery (I'm not even going to mention her feelings about incest) but because her body was exposed for all to see.

"Shame. Shame. Shame."

Before we really dive into shame, I want you to know there is such a thing as "healthy shame," which is connected to modesty, humility, gratitude, and a respect for self and others It's been seen as a powerful motivation for personal growth and change, and in constructing meaningful and congenial relationships (Ng, 2020). This is often present in non-western cultures. I will caution, however, that healthy shame can be easily warped into maladaptive shame and quickly become dehumanizing. I will also say that the word shame is kind of a buzzword right now, maybe even overused at times, but I am thankful that there is attention being paid to it as it can be detrimental for many.

In the DSM-5, a manual that psychotherapists use for diagnosing, shame was recently added to the diagnostic criteria for PTSD under the broad function of "persistent negative emotional states" (Taylor, 2015). Accordingly, shame has recently been seen in trauma literature as part of an assemblage of negative emotions. Already in this category is fear, horror, anger and guilt – all of which are common for trauma survivors in a state of post-trauma.

Purity culture and shame are so woven together, it is hard to see anything but an intricate tapestry when you look at the concepts. Indeed, purity culture needed shame to flourish. It relied on shame to keep purity alive. One thing that purity culture forgot, however, was the concept that "you cannot shame or belittle people into changing their behaviors" (Brown, p.1, 2007). Brown's research found that shame can temporarily change behaviors, but that these changes are rarely long-lasting. Still, people tend to build large parts of their lives around shame. At all levels – individual, familial, societal – shame is used to try to change others and to protect ourselves. What is often missed is how shame ends up disconnecting us from our soul, spirit, and relationships.

Shame is one of those things that, until recently, was not discussed until the rise of the blessed mother Brene Brown. That has been mind-blowing for me, and yet, I was one of those people that was too ashamed to truly share my own story connected to shame. Brene Brown, the world's greatest shame researcher, used qualitative data to develop a conceptual definition of shame: "Shame is the intensely painful feeling or experience of believing we are flawed and therefore unworthy of acceptance and belonging" (p.5, 2007). When I look at that definition, I cannot help but be pulled back to those highly intensive moments at church camp or youth groups where it was taught that to be sexually impure would lead to being unworthy. In this way, shame took hold in so many of us when we were just kids.

Where Shame Starts

Humans are typically born without self-conscious emotions present (such as shame, pride, or guilt), but these emotions begin showing up as a child develops a sense of self. This typically happens around 18-24 months of age (Lewis, 2007). Before this point in development, children can experience emotions such as joy and happiness, but self-evaluative emotions are not present. As a child nears the age of three, they can begin to recognize themselves in a mirror and will start to form thoughts about their physical body. According to Griffin (1995), by the age of eight, children will begin to develop the understanding of social standards, recognize violations, and be aware of a judgmental audience, all of which are essential components of experiencing shame and guilt.

A major influence of the shame experience of children is related to parenting and the parent-child attachment bond. These bonds can be classified as secure, avoidant, anxious, or disorganized. Secure attachment is this wonderful thing that every child needs to have with their caregiver in order to feel safe in relationships and safe enough to explore the world around them. Children need attachment to survive (and adults need it to). Attachment theory suggests that the quality of early childhood relationships (between a child and a caregiver) significantly impacts the mental representations, expectations, and beliefs that a child will develop as it relates to a sense of "self" and to others (Bowlby, 1983).

Children tend to internalize the attitude that parents' have towards their children, so one could suppose that if parents are critical or demanding, then children will inevitably view themselves in a negative light or be quick to criticize themselves. Additionally, research shows that when treatment of children by parents is harsh or critical, or when abuse is present, a child will draw the conclusion that they are unwanted or undesirable, which ultimately leads to shame (Bennett, Sullivan, and Lewis, 2005). Past research found that a child's memory of being put-down, non-favored, and belittled by parents during formative years is related to shame-proneness or a likelihood of being impacted by shame in adulthood (Gilbert, Allan, and Goss, 1996). All this to say, shame can start at quite a young age and is impacted by early attachments and parental factors. This is compounded by the theory that some people are more predisposed to shame than others.

As a child ages and begins to have a sense of right or wrong, social acceptability, whether they fit in or not, they will also likely learn the cultural norms and "rules" they should comply with to stay in a state of social belonging. When a person begins to become aware of the discrepancies between who they are and who they think they should be, shame can take hold or, if it's already there, deepen. When we consider purity culture and all the rules and norms related to how a person should be (in this case its scripts about sexuality) and who they really are (a sexual being, one who doesn't fit the mold), this is where sexual shame begins.

Sexual Shame

To me, sexual shame is one of the ultimate dividers between a person and a sense of wholeness. Sexual shame has been defined as "A visceral feeling of humiliation and disgust toward one's own body and identity as a sexual being and a belief of being abnormal and inferior; this feeling can be internalized but also manifests in interpersonal relationships having a negative on trust, communication, and physical and emotional intimacy" (Clarke, p. 87 2017). A result of purity culture's emphasis on appropriate and inappropriate behaviors in conjunction with religious values and teachings is that many youth, like me, took those messages as right/wrong behavior resulting in either/or thinking. From this, a fear arose that others would find out what happened to me, and shame for feeling like the outlier began to creep in. Despite my early sexual experiences being non-consensual, I still believed I had engaged in sinful and wrong behavior. I believed I could have prevented it. In the moments when I am not able to reconcile my unwanted sexual experiences with religious messaging, I feel sexual shame.

Purity culture amplified and eternized scripts of inferiority, self-denial, objectification, and shame resulting in dysfunction being present in multiple areas of life even beyond sexuality. Klein (2018) reflected, "We (those in purity culture) went to war with ourselves, our own bodies, and our own sexual natures," which led to intense guilt, shame, and incomprehension of how to have safe and pleasurable sexual encounters. Said another way, we were taught in the name of religion to attack ourselves, our sacredness as women, and to try to amputate a natural and life-giving part of our being. The disconnection began for me when I was sixteen years old with that first fracture between my mind and my body. My mind could not stop thinking of how I was ruined and how I would be unwanted for the rest of my life. I stopped believing that me or my body were worthy of safety and softness. The "intimacy" that I could engage in was shallow, manipulative, and impulsive, and it continued to carve out the already hollow spaces in my body.

The more the message of shame was reinforced in my body by my actions, the further I tried to leave my body behind. Often ruminating on thoughts such as: *do not be present with it, it can only be used by others, you can't trust any sense of real connection.* This was sexual shame that showed up as symptoms of trauma being enacted in my everyday life, and this, ultimately, was the impact. I lost any sense of connection with my essence. My body became nothing but something to be used, and I felt it was only good for being used. Every use took me away from whatever sense of worth I had and any alignment with spirituality. It made me feel shame and less than in relationships. It convinced me that when I had to "confess" my sexual immorality to the good Christian boy I would (later) marry, his face would contort into disgust, and I would be that rose with all the petals peeled off we learned about in youth group.

I still remember how loud my heart was pounding when I had the conversation (the one where I told him I thought I was a slut) while we were walking on his Christian college campus. I remember the relief when he told me it didn't matter and that he wasn't going anywhere. I sometimes think he should have turned tail and run! Because sexual shame in combination with sexual trauma has made marriage quite complicated at times. What has stuck with me is that in therapy I have heard the impact of my own sexual shame story reflected in the stories of my clients. In a way, it was incredibly validating to realize my story wasn't unique and that women (and men) who haven't experienced sexual trauma but did grow up in purity culture have had the same sexual functioning hang ups that I have had.

Shame Within the Body

In psychology, when we are first meeting a person for therapy, we look for the impact of symptoms from a biological, psychological, sociological, and spiritual standpoint. The hope is that we can capture the whole experience of a person and see how their pain is impacting multiple areas of their life. This, in turn, informs the treatment plan and the goals of therapy.

Before we move on, I must confess something. I'm still feeling vulnerable as I write this. I've checked in with myself to be curious of whether vulnerability is showing up as shame or something else. I've landed on noticing I am feeling vulnerable with you reading about me and my sexuality (see – purity culture is still around), but I am deciding to add some of my story in this next section. It's not a full "ladies tell all," but I will be weaving my own experiences into the information and stories I'll share with you as we look at how sexual shame impacts multiple areas of life.

Gender Considerations

As we all know, everyone experiences shame to some degree throughout their lifetime. We do know that women process shame differently than men. Specifically, a woman's experience of shame often relates to who they *should* be, how they *should* be, and what they *should* be (Brown, 2008). Women tend to have more intense feelings of shame from the negative evaluations of self (think back to the last chapter where self-objectification was mentioned). One author has hypothesized that there are three reasons women feel more shame than men: 1) there is active shaming and silencing of women by the patriarchy; 2) women tend to be more open about their desire for connection and therefore vulnerable when experiencing a broken connection; and 3) women tend to feel they have let others down or been a burden in interpersonal relationships (Jordan, 1997).

When we think about the societal and personal pressures women (and men) face, it's easy to see that women tend to have a sense of "being wrong" more than "doing wrong." When women continually experience a sense of their very being as wrong, shame steps in, which leads to a sense of disempowerment and, ultimately, silences the needs and wants of women. It seems women spend their lives denying themselves needs and wants – desire and pleasure – by dividing themselves into pieces that are taken by others or pieces that we thought we needed permission to acknowledge. When we are divided into pieces, we are easier to control – whether it is by shame, damaging purity standards, or our own internalized critical beliefs.

> There are questions I have asked myself over the years and have also heard from my clients, typical female clients, but not always:
>
> What if I want something "bad" – what if what I like about it, is that it feels bad?
>
> Am I supposed to have desire? Isn't that wrong?
>
> I don't even know my own body. Thinking of anything "down there" grosses me out.
>
> Aren't desire and pleasure wrong?
>
> Why can't I orgasm?
>
> Why do I want sex and he/she doesn't? What does that mean?

These questions have an underlying fear that "something is wrong with me." With so many questions, and often nowhere to turn, individuals will internalize this feeling of wrongness and begin to avoid sex and sexuality altogether because of the shame stemming from fear. When we think about messages from purity culture, typically passages from the Bible taken out of context, these messages will reinforce a feeling of shame. Think about those passages where the first humans had to cover their genitals from shame, or hearing that you have a heart that is "deceitfully wicked above all things."

Think about the message that what you want is wrong and you are wrong for wanting it, or that your pleasure and desire are the opposite of "dying to self." To comply, we let parts of ourselves die.

In the majority of modern research when sexual shame and gender is mentioned the automatic has been to see sexual shame as a woman's issue. Often, the male experience is left out of the conversation, but research found several male sexual concerns that can be sources of shame, including things such as solo sex (i.e. masturbation) and use of sexually explicit materials, sexual experience, sexual inexperience, body dissatisfaction, sexual ability concerns, and sexual libido (Gordon, 2017). This could be in part due to the sexual and gender scripts that come from purity culture, and at times society at large, regarding traditional masculine ideals that promote an assertive, always capable, skilled sexuality ideal. Men may experience the inability to live up to internalized gender and sexual ideals as shame (Gordon, 2019). It is incredibly sad to think that the traditional messaging to boys and men has been to be the pursuer, which takes away the chance to experience being the object of desire or even to have and acknowledge intimate relationships with other men. It is sad that traditional messaging privileges casual sex over deep connection. The confusion that occurs due to shutting off natural parts of our humanity to ascribe to a script that is outdated and leads to disconnection from others and our emotions is difficult and unhealthy for us all.

Regardless of gender identity, I find comfort in the words of Carole Shadbolt (2009 p.166) who said, "Our sexual selves and our experiences of our bodies in relationship to other bodies (as well as our own) are as diverse as the human face – not one in all the world is exactly the same. Like our faces, our sexuality is fluid and has a myriad of expressions and reactions... Our sexualities, like our faces, are unique, multifaceted, shifting, deeply relational two-way mirrors."

Mental Health

Shame is found to be linked to many mental health diagnoses as well as sexual dysfunction disorders. I want to note that I am speaking generally about shame and not specifically about sexual shame. Some of the mental health diagnoses include anxiety, depression, eating disorders, and PTSD.

Shame can often be a primary precipitating factor related to the onset of a diagnosis, and it can also be an emotion that inflames specific mental health symptoms.

When shame is present, a person is likely to have anxious and depressive thoughts. Typically, this will include negative self-evaluations and self-talk that includes high levels of self-criticism or contempt. Depression is commonly associated with a decrease in sense of self, which, in turn, leads to shame about who we are or just feeling lost. Anxiety is often related to using a disparaging and harsh lens when recalling situations and feeling intense shame when something is said or done that could be considered "wrong." A common symptom of depression and anxiety is *rumination* (where a thought gets stuck on repeat in your mind). Let me tell you – rumination and shame are the worst kind of friends.

When we replay a moment over and over in our minds, we experience continued increased levels of shame. Sexual shame could look something like recalling past sexual experiences with self-criticism related to sexual functioning, the "breaking" of purity vows, or even feeling like you caused an unwanted sexual interaction. The more we replay what we think was "wrong," the more distressed we typically become, especially when looking at the past with contempt rather than compassion. I'm picturing a client sitting across from me who is struggling with having an orgasm with her partner. One of the barriers is that when this person is being sexually stimulated, they are recalling an experience of "hooking up" with another person when they were a teenager. Now, they are consumed with shame regarding this instance, which makes it difficult to be present in the moment and hinders her from achieving orgasm.

Shame is also a central component to the feelings one has about their bodies. For instance, most media portray women as beautiful when they are underweight, leading to setting dangerous expectations for women. All women (myself included) fall into the trap of comparing the body they have with the one they are "supposed" to have. Not meeting these expectations, despite being completely outrageous, can cause shame to arise. From here, a person is more susceptible to begin restricting, dieting, or compulsively exercising to try to meet these ridiculous expectations. When these types of behavior take hold in our bodies, we are likely to develop disordered eating patterns that create a new space for shame to live.

High self-criticism and hostility are often found in the eating disorder population. Those with eating disorders will fervently shame themselves through negative self-evaluation and the pursuit of thinness. Recent statistics state that eating disorders affect around 5-10% of adolescent males and 2% of adult males, so this is not just a female issue (Trompeter, Bussey, and Mitchison, 2021). We used to think that only women were comparing themselves to unattainable standards of body image, but the research reveals that this is simply inaccurate. As mentioned, body dissatisfaction is a symptom of most eating disorders. When the beauty standard for men is that they are muscular, tall, and have a full head of hair, they just as easily fall into the trap of comparison and self-shame. Body shame can cause any of us to disconnect from ourselves and our intuition about what we want and what we need. We silence our own voice, and we silence our longing for basic needs.

In addition to body image issues, shame also shows up in diagnostic criteria for post-traumatic stress disorder (PTSD). Specifically, PTSD includes an ongoing negative emotional state, which includes shame. This is due to a traumatic event, typically being something an individual could not help with, fix, or stop. Having intrusive and distressing memories about the trauma is quite typical but often leads people to believe they were weak or caused the trauma, and this is where shame plays a role because shame can lead to an intensification of symptoms. I want to note, here, that living with shame has been devastating for me. I, just like many survivors of sexual assault, replay memories again and again looking for all the ways I "could have/should have stopped it." And, while this shame has quieted over the years, it is still living in my bones. Indeed, there were times of transition and change that felt out of my control and unpredictable – moving across the country, being constantly evaluated, becoming a parent – where it felt like I had no legs to stand on. It is during these times that I once again discover my mind returning to those traumatic memories and trying to find some control of a situation that cannot be altered.

Sexuality

Some research suggests that shame is impacted by sexuality more than any other factor (Hastings, 1998). Of course, shame impacts sexuality – it's why I'm writing this book and why you're reading it. Kyle (2013) defined sexual shame as an "intensely painful feeling or experience of believing we are flawed and therefore unworthy of acceptance and belonging due to our current or past sexual thoughts, or experiences, or behaviors." Others suggest that sexual shame refers to the deep responsibility and weighty remorse associated with participation in and thoughts/fantasies about sexual intimacy or activity (Clark, 2017). It is the intense feeling of being flawed and unworthy of acceptance and belonging that most concerns us here because this belief that who we are is bad leaks into our ability to connect to ourselves and hinders our ability to explore and own our sexuality. It also skews our ability to be vulnerable enough to share it with another person(s).

My own story caused shame to morph into particular things for me, such as the feeling that I have to be engaged sexually because I am less than and owe something to another person. The cost of that thinking is high, but it remains strong within me. I can shake it off from time to time, but at other times, it gets knotted up and feels impossible to untangle. While I am thinking of my story when it comes to sexual shame, I have also born witness to others who felt similarly. Over the years people in my life say things such as:

"I feel like I am just here to get him (partner) off."

"I feel so disconnected. I can't actually be in-the-moment when we are having sex."

"I don't want to be touched anywhere. I get so anxious that I can't really feel anything."

"I feel so uncomfortable there is no way I can even get close to having an orgasm."

"I've never orgasmed, is something wrong with me?"

"Every time we have (penetrative) sex, it's painful. But it feels like I can't say no."

"Sometimes I think about wanting to be more dominant, but that feels like it might be wrong."

Many of these expressions are, again, a result of purity culture. It shaped us to believe we shouldn't know our own bodies. It taught us that pleasure is not part of sex, women don't have autonomy when it comes to their bodies, and there is a "right way" to express sexuality. I want to hone in on some specific ways that shame can impact sexuality, especially for women.

One of these is something known as subtle coercion. This refers to sexual pressure that is often unconscious but greatly impacts how a partner can sexually communicate with another. This pressure can show up as a perceived pressure to respond to and satisfy a partners' needs, to be the always ready supplier of sex, and to conform to the sexual scripts that purity culture gave women. Again, sexual scripts often involved the objectification of the female partner. One study found that, typically, if a woman perceives her male partner as objectifying her, then they are significantly more likely to believe part of gender/purity scripting that it is a woman's role to satisfy male needs for sex (Ramsey and Hoyt, 2015). Additionally, this study found that perceived objectification is linked to a higher likelihood of experiencing "sexual coercion in general and sexual coercion via commitment manipulation" (Ramsey and Hoyt, 2015, p. 161). Sexual coercion is also a result of hetero (traditional) sexual scripts that state men are sexual initiators who are open to and pursue any sexual opportunity and rarely take no for an answer. The same script says that women are sexually reluctant gatekeepers of men (Hartwick, et. al., 2007).

I realize I am using language that assumes all women are the victims of sexual coercion, and I want to acknowledge that is not true. Anyone can be a victim and can be impacted by sexual coercion, regardless of gender identity. However, research consistently finds that significantly more women than men experience sexual coercion and that significantly more men than women perpetrate or use sexual coercion. This interplay of coercion is crucial to understand my overall point because shame plays into this experience. Shame influences the way that sexual and gender scripts from purity culture set individuals up to follow these scripts, and it affects the ways we come to believe we are doing something wrong if we deviate from the script. These scripts can cause individuals to engage in sexual experiences with partners out of obligation, which isn't always full consent. This is one manifestation of subtle coercion, and the result can look like symptoms of trauma, such as the inability to be present (dissociation), the feeling of lack of agency, disconnection from one's body, and self-blame. To be clear, these are not results that are indicative of consent or trust, and as we know intuitively, coercion is never about consent or trust.

Another way shame can impact sexuality is through dissociation. Dissociation is generally viewed as a disruption in consciousness, identity, memory and/or perception. It is often a symptom of PTSD, but it can be experienced by those who have not been traumatized and is expressed through derealization (feeling a disconnect from reality) and depersonalization (feeling disconnected from one's body). Dissociation can be looked at as your mind's way of trying to protect you from re-traumatization. Sexual dissociation is experienced predominantly by those who experienced sexual abuse in childhood or as an adult, but it can also impact those with no experience of sexual abuse. Sexual dissociation can look like having trouble stopping your mind from wandering while intimate with a partner, feeling disconnected from your body during sex, not being able to feel bodily sensations during sex, and difficulty having an emotional connection with a partner (Travers, 2022). When this occurs, it could be interpreted as your body or mind trying to tell you something.

When it occurs for me, it is when I fall into the purity trap of it being my responsibility to care for the needs of a man. I start to feel as if I am confined in a space that does not feel safe for my being. My body is smart and has protected me many times throughout the years by helping me not to have memories of some traumas and giving me intuition that guides me. In this same vein, when it senses I am doing something I don't fully want to do, it goes into protection mode and draws a line between my body and what is happening. This is something that is less frequent in my life as I have learned to listen more closely to my body and to communicate with my partner about my needs, but it still points to a very real and uncomfortable experience of sexual dysfunction.

Recent research specifically highlights how shame can impact sexual dysfunction in females. There are three main female dysfunction diagnoses in the field of psychology: female orgasmic disorder, female sexual interest/arousal disorder, and genito-pelvic pain/penetration disorder (GPPPD) formerly known as vaginismus. Female orgasmic disorder is exactly as it sounds. It is defined as having difficulty achieving orgasm and/or having a significant reduction in intensity or orgasmic sensation (APA, 2022). It may be helpful to know that it's the second most prevalent female sexual dysfunction (Kingsberg et al., 2013). A 2016 study found that 48% of females struggled to achieve orgasm 50% of the time during partnered sex (Rowland and Kolba, 2016). While it's helpful to know, it doesn't paint a full picture as some women have no problem achieving orgasm when masturbating but struggle to do so with a partner, or vice versa. In what feels like a cruel twist of fate, the more shame or distress that is felt in not achieving orgasm, the harder it becomes to orgasm.

Sexual interest can be thought of as sexual feelings or drives that give us the motivation to participate in a sexual encounter with a partner or unaccompanied. Sexual arousal is physical or mental readiness for sexual activity, and it's measured by physiological changes that take place in the body such as increased genital or nongenital sensations (APA, 2022). Low sexual desire is the most prevalent female sexual dysfunction, affecting one in every three women (Bancroft et al., 2003; Rosen et al., 2009). I want to say this loud and clear for the people in the back...*roughly 33% of women struggle with sexual desire*. That does not mean you don't care about your partner or that you are not a sexual being. It does not mean that something is "wrong" with you. The percentage of women who experience low sexual desire speaks to something beyond any individual deficit.

Genito-pelvic pain/penetration disorder (GPPPD) used to be known as vaginismus or dyspareunia. There are several markers for this diagnosis including: difficulty with vaginal penetration during sex, genito-pelvic pain (this is where the pelvic muscles around the vagina contract and/or tighten whenever penetration is attempted), fear of pain or anxiety related to penetrative intercourse, or contraction or tension of pelvic floor muscles when attempting penetrative sex (APA, 2022). There are no concrete numbers regarding what percent of women experience this, but what is noted in research is that 60% of women who experience GPPPD report that it impacts their ability to enjoy life, especially if partners are wanting to become pregnant (Arnold et al., 2006; Sadownik et al., 2017). Shame and GPPPD are interconnected in that many women go undiagnosed or misdiagnosed for years before receiving an official diagnosis. Some women will go to a gynecologist and be told they need to relax, or just try to have more sex, or have a glass of something to "loosen up" before sex. All these responses tend to create the idea that it is a person's fault that pain is present in their body, and they often truly believe this until they are correctly diagnosed. For many women, it is a feat in and of itself to be willing to discuss sexual concerns with a doctor. This may be due to embarrassment or fear, especially those women living with purity culture ideas/messages who are told to ignore or be silent about sexuality. In addition, the medical field is not always the kindest to women and often invalidates female pain.

One last thing I want to mention, here, is how shame can snuff out a sense of play in sexuality. I'm using the word play because it brings to mind the feeling I would have when I would play outside as a kid. The scene in my head is one where I'm running around with friends, it's the perfect day (sunny and breezy), I don't have a care in the world, and I am incredibly happy. There is no shame. I'm just free and having the time of my life! There is a lot of research out there discussing why play is so important for development in children, but then, it seems like we get to a certain point and think it's not needed in adulthood. Playing as an adult boosts overall well-being, increases creativity, decreases mental distress, improves your physical health, and helps us to find new parts of our personalities. Research is catching up on all this, and there is now even the *Journal of Play in Adulthood*, which seeks to help us find more information about the needs and benefits of play and playfulness in adulthood. One major benefit is that playfulness is not shame-based, and this means that sexual play can be very healing for those struggling with sexual shame.

One type of sexual play involves sexual kinks. Stay with me here, I know kink can feel like a "sinful" or taboo word, and it really doesn't have to be. Sexual kinks encompass a broad spectrum or sexual acts or interests that are considered to be non-mainstream. Some examples of mainstream sexual acts are, but are not limited to, penis-vaginal intercourse, oral sex, or manual stimulation (that means using your hands). Sexual behaviors not considered mainstream are, again not limited to, role-playing, breath-play (choking), impact-play (spanking), fetishes, or BDSM (erotic practices involving dominance, submissiveness, masochism or sadomasochism). Some sexual play is more widely accepted than others, such as using sex toys or anal sex, and it shows us that sexual play exists on a spectrum that is subjective. Now, as I said, play is not shame-based, but shame can certainly prevent us from engaging in play in the first place. Shame almost always keeps people from exploring a sexually playful side of themselves, and purity culture often perpetuates the idea that anything outside of mainstream sexual expression is wrong. So, when we have desires that align more with sexual play or kink, we can shame ourselves into silence, thinking that we are wrong for wanting certain experiences.

Interpersonal Patterns

Shame plays a significant role in many relational dynamics. Specifically, it moves us away from one another in an attempt to create a false sense of safety. In relationships, we might feel shame when we are seen by others as flawed in some pivotal way (this can be in reality or some imagined scenario of memory) or when some core aspect of ourselves is seen as inadequate, immoral, or infelicitous. Continual experiences of shame can eventually solidify into shame-proneness, which is the tendency to view and experience our core self or our entire personhood as inherently flawed, bad, defective, and unworthy (Tangney, 1996).

Shame-proneness can be particularly painful and is often incapacitating when a person feels inferior to others, hopeless, or helpless. In fact, it will often determine they need to hide personal flaws from those they are in relationships with (Andrews et al., 2002). When we are feeling like we are unworthy, we end up in a state of high alert, trying to remain safe in relationships. We start to hide, cutting off our thoughts, passions, and emotional vulnerability essentially trying to escape rejection. But rejection is already there in the form of self-rejection and intimacy rejection. Beyond just hiding or withdrawing from others, we can choose to attack them. If we can hurt someone first, then perhaps they will not be strong enough to hurt us. In these ways, shame keeps us from truly engaging in the magic of being connected to another human being at a deep level.

Spirituality

Spirituality to me is about the connection I have to all the parts of myself, with others, and with a Higher Power – in my case, God. We know that shame is the ultimate disconnector, and it separates us and isolates us. Shame destroys relationships, wellbeing, and our self-image. It leads us to hide from ourselves and our God. Maybe this looks like leaving the church or deconstructing without reconstructing. Or, maybe it means constantly feeling like you have to "do more" to be worthy, keeping us hustling to rid the fear of rejection we have.

For me, shame erected a wall between myself and God. Beyond the image I held of God in childhood, I honestly felt like I let God down by getting assaulted. I had to make things right, and when I couldn't do this, when my mind and body were unable to heal, I felt like I was inadequate. So, to avoid the pain, I pushed myself away from God. Now, I still went to church. I volunteered with the youth group, I sang, and I prayed, but it felt like I was doing all of this just so I would not be cast out by God. I was so afraid, and that fear eventually turned to bitterness and anger.

Why would God let all these things happen to me? Why was God not present when I needed help? I hated the shame that crawled through me. Shame is rarely warranted, and in my case, I know now that it was not. But when we are so deep in a pit of shame, we cannot see light, we cannot breathe, and it feels as if there is no use in trying to climb out.

What Now?

I wonder if you got to the end of this chapter and you were thinking – *thanks so much Esther for writing about all of the ways that shame impacts a person because I now feel worse than I did before reading this chapter.* But that was the point. The point was to see how shame impacts a person! I wanted to validate that all these things we experience – mental health concerns, sexual dysfunction, shame, confusion in sex – these things do not mean you are wrong. We do not have to feel worse. This chapter can show us that wrong things have been done to us. It can reveal that the messages that break us and cause us to retreat within ourselves are no longer true. We do not need to internalize any of this shit anymore, and we can actually be free. So, what does this freedom look like? I wonder how a fully connected human (a soul, body, and mind) truly lives? I wonder what they feel? I wonder how this reconnection happens and if it's meant for us?

Get Curious

1. Can you recall the first time you felt shame? What message did you conclude from that experience?

2. How do you think shame impacts your relationship with yourself and others? Are there other spaces you feel shame disconnect you from the world around you?

3. How does shame impact your sexuality?

4. If you started to see sex as playful – what would it look like?

5. If you did not experience shame, what would your relationships, wellbeing, sexuality, and spirituality be like?

Chapter Two References

American Psychiatric Association (2022). *Diagnostic and statistical manual of mental disorders* (5th ed., text rev.). doi: 10.1176/appi. books.9781585624836.jb13.

Andrews, B., Qian, M., & Valentine, J. D. (2002). Predicting depressive symptoms with a new measure of shame: the experience of shame scale. *The British Journal of Clinical Psychology*, 41(Pt 1), 29–42. doi: 10.1348/014466502163778.

Arnold, L. D., Bachmann, G. A., Rosen, R., Kelly, S., & Rhoads, G. G. (2006). Vulvodynia: characteristics and associations with comorbidities and quality of life. *Obstetrics and Gynecology*, 107(3), 617–624. doi: 10.1097/01.AOG.0000199951.26822.27.

Bancroft, J., Loftus, J., & Long, J. S. (2003). Distress about sex: a national survey of women in heterosexual relationships. *Archives of Sexual Behavior*, 32(3), 193–208. doi: 10.1023/a:1023420431760.

Bennett, D. S., Sullivan, M. W., & Lewis, M. (2005). Young children's adjustment as a function of maltreatment, shame, and anger. *Child Maltreatment*, 4, 311-323.

Bowlby, J. (1983). *Attachment*. Attachment and loss, Vol. 1. Basic Books.

Brown, B. (2008). *I thought it was just me (but it isn't): Making the journey from "what will people think?" to "I am enough."* Gotham.

Clark, N. (2017). *The etiology and phenomenology of sexual shame: A grounded theory study* [Ph.D., Seattle Pacific University].

Gordon, A. (2017). How men experience sexual shame: the development and validation of the male sexual shame scale (MSSS). *The Journal of Men's Studies*, 26(1): 105-123.

Gordon, A. (2019). Male sexual shame, masculinity, and mental health. *New Male Studies: An International Journal*, 8(1): 1-24.

Griffin, S. (1995). A cognitive-developmental analysis of pride, shame, and embarrassment in middle childhood. In J.P. Tangney & K. W. Fischer (Eds.), *Self-conscious emotions: the psychology of shame, guilt, embarrassment, and pride* (pp. 219-236). The Guilford Press.

Hartwick C., Desmarais S., & Hennig K. (2007). Characteristics of male and female victims of sexual coercion. *Canadian Journal of Human Sexuality*, 16, 31-44.

Hastings, A. S. (1998). *Treating sexual shame: A new map for overcoming dysfunction, abuse, and addiction.* Jason Aronson.

Jordan, J. (1997) Relational development: Therapeutic implications for empathy and shame. In J. Jordan (Ed.), *Women's growth in diversity: More writings from the stone center.* The Guilford Press.

Kingsberg, S. A., Wysocki, S., Magnus, L., & Krychman, M. L. (2013). Vulvar and vaginal atrophy in postmenopausal women: findings from the REVIVE (REal Women's VIews of Treatment Options for Menopausal Vaginal ChangEs) survey. *The Journal of Sexual Medicine*, 10(7), 1790–1799. doi: 10.1111/jsm.12190.

Kyle, S. E. (2013). Identification and treatment of sexual shame: development of a measurement tool and group therapy protocol. (Unpublished Doctoral Dissertation) *American Academy of Clinical Sexologists.* San Antonio, TX.

Lewis, M. (2007). Self-conscious emotional development. In J. L. Tracy, R.W. Robins, & J. P. Tangney (Eds.), *The self-conscious emotions: theory and research* (pp. 134-149). The Guilford Press.

Ng., E. (2020). *Shame-informed counseling and psychotherapy: eastern and western perspectives.* Routledge.

Ramsey, L. R. & Hoyt, T. (2015). The object of desire: how being objectified creates sexual pressure for women in heterosexual relationships. *Psychology of Women Quarterly*, 39(2), 151–170. doi: 10.1177/0361684314544679.

Rosen, R. C., Bachmann, G. A., Reese, J. B., Gentner, L., Leiblum, S., Wajszczuk, C., & Wanser, R. (2009). Female sexual well-being scale (FSWB scale): development and psychometric validation in sexually functional women. *The Journal of Sexual Medicine*, 6(5), 1297–1305. doi: 10.1111/j.1743-6109.2009.01240.x.

Rowland, D. L. & Kolba, T. N. (2016). Understanding orgasmic difficulty in women. *The Journal of Sexual Medicine*, 13(8), 1246–1254. doi: 10.1016/j.jsxm.2016.05.014.

Sadownik, L. A., Smith, K. B., Hui, A., & Brotto, L. A. (2017). The Impact of a woman's dyspareunia and its treatment on her intimate partner: A qualitative analysis. *Journal of Sex & Marital Therapy*, 43(6), 529–542. doi: 10.1080/0092623X.2016.1208697.

Shadbolt, C. (2009). Sexuality and shame. *Transactional Analysis Journal*, 39(2), 163–172. doi: 10.1177/036215370903900210.

Tangney, J. P. (1996). Conceptual and methodological issues in the assessment of shame and guilt. *Behaviour Research and Therapy*, 34(9), 741-754. doi: 10.1016/0005- 7967(96)00034-4.

Taylor, T. F. (2015). The influence of shame on posttrauma disorders: Have we failed to see the obvious? *European Journal of Psychotraumatology*, 6(1) doi: 10.3402/ejpt.v6.28847.

Tomkins, S. S. (1987). Shame. In D. L. Nathainson (Ed.), *The many faces of shame* (pp. 133-161). The Guilford Press.

Travers, M. (2022). Two ways to manage dissociation during sex. *Psychology Today Online*, retrieved July 29, 2023 from https://www.psychologytoday.com/us/blog/social-instincts/202211/2-ways-manage-dissociation-during-sex.

Trompeter, N., Bussey, K., & Mitchison, D. (2021). Epidemiology of eating disorders in boys and men. In Nagata, J.M., Brown, T.A., Murray, S.B., & Lavender, J.M. (Eds.), *Eating disorders in boys and men*. Springer. doi: 10.1007/978-3-030-67127-3_4.

Chapter Three

Reclaiming the Self

Shame is a major obstacle in living a life that is joyful, pleasurable, and purposeful. It is devastatingly destructive and exclusively a human trait because it is indicative of self-consciousness. Shame likely existed since the Stone Ages when belonging to a tribe was a matter of survival. If one didn't belong, then it would ultimately mean death as reliance upon one another was key to living. This sentiment is the same for us now. We need to know we belong and that we are worthy. We need relationships and connection or we do not carry on.

We all carry sexual shame to some degree. Sometimes it is quite subtle or unconscious, and with others, it can be overt. Maybe you even notice your whole body becoming tense just by hearing the word sex. Sexual shame can be related to how a body, or specifically genitals appear, whether someone has "too much experience" or "not enough experience", sexual desires, kinks, and fantasies. Or the one I often hear about in therapy is shame related to bodily fluids and sounds of pleasure that are often made during sexual encounters.

Sexuality is the most puissant form of life energy. Sexuality is the force by which you and I came into being and it's the force by which we create new life. Sexuality is the genesis of health, happiness, passion, power, playfulness, and pleasure. Sexuality is one of the most powerful connectors we have to our own body and one of the most intimate connections we can have with another human being. For many, sexuality was obtuse, traded for conditional love, or painful, but it has the ability to be the ultimate declaration of self-love. Why? Because it provokes you to express yourself. Whether it's how we show up in the proverbial bedroom or how we show up in the world around us.

In the pages to follow, we will explore some of the ways we can begin to inhabit the full expression of our sexual being. We will explore ways in which we can begin to re-author and re-frame our own story and how we can invite others in the authoring as well. At times, I hope you pause and engage with some of the exercises. I say this because it is really easy to read something and think, *I'll come back to it.* That never works for me. I have so many books with dog-eared pages just waiting for me to come back. So, really slow down and take all the time you desire. While you read, I also invite you to hold onto the thought that to connect with your body and with your sexuality is an act of rebellion against purity culture, and sometimes being a rebel can feel pretty damn good.

Belonging to Yourself

Part of this rebellion involves doing the opposite of many messages the world gives to people based on gender, race, or religious/political beliefs. The world frames belonging as related to the people or environment around you leading you to abandon your own internal experiences and authentic self for the prize of "fitting in." Brene Brown (2010) says that true belonging can only occur when we show up as our authentic and imperfect self and that our sense of belonging can't be greater than our ability to accept ourselves.

What if instead of just accepting ourselves we take it a step further and become an untiring advocate for ourselves? It is alright to be dedicated to caring and nurturing the spirit, body, and mind. Oftentimes, we are taught to put others before ourselves or to "turn the other cheek." I'm not sure that's really working for us anymore. Part of who I am is someone who can love very loyally and can see and work to meet the needs of others. What I want is to have that same ability directed at myself with the same passion and zeal – if not more! However, I can't truly advocate for myself if I don't know who I am; If I feel like I have to hide. We can only fully embrace who we are when we celebrate, or at the very least accept, the qualities that are intrinsically our own.

So, what keeps you from showing up fully as your imperfect, messy, beautiful self? Shame? Fear? The voice in your head that sounds like your mom or your ex or your old pastor? It's time to strengthen our own voices – rock the boat – figure out who we are and truly honor and accept ourselves. We have the power to own our choices, values, desires regardless of how others may perceive us. This means you have to show up for yourself. You have to risk the (sometimes) painful process of self-discovery and self-awareness. Start to educate you about you! As we've looked at earlier in this book, our identities are formed by disinformation and misinformation about the identities we hold. We don't have to keep acting in ways that reinforce the biased opinions we were sold as truth. To unlearn the bias taught to us throughout life we have to re-educate ourselves about what is actually true for us. Societal structures and scripts weigh down humanity through strategies of exclusion and oppression, but we can unlearn our ways of existing within those structures.

Some of the misinformation I internalized was that I had no power, I needed to stay quiet, I was a stupid person, I needed to smile when I wasn't happy, I should care for others' comfort above my own, even if the cost was emotionally high. I also learned that I should avoid conflict at all costs, and I should swallow the words that would dismantle those in power who crush others in an effort to remain at the top. These were the societal lies that kept me from belonging to myself.

Recently, and with great love and support by many in my life, I am truly believing that I can belong to myself. I feel excited to figure out who I really am. I think I'm outrageous (in a good way) under all the shit I've been buried under. I am expecting to find power that I have never considered myself to have, and I will find the legs to stand on that were tucked under me for so long. Part of my self-discovery of belonging led me to rocking the boat in different spaces of my life, and let me tell you, what and who needs to go overboard will and those who love you won't be going anywhere. By not conforming to who I was "supposed" to be, I was able to finally feel at home within myself. It came at a cost though. I had to leave things that felt safe and realize the truth about those who couldn't see all the true and precious parts of me. This process of finding me helped me to realize I deserve to be seen and to be heard and to be known for all the parts of me.

So, what will be your truth – your story? You are the main character, the author, the editor. This life is your story, and when you belong to yourself, you are the only one that gets to tell the story. You decide what is good and what is true. No one else. Life showed me that when I am fragmented and disconnected from myself, I can more easily be controlled and lost from myself. Our emotions are stolen. We are trapped in cycles of measuring our bodies making sure we meet someone else's expectations. We self-objectify, and we change our sense of worth multiple times in a day. This rejection of a true self robs us of passion, of our beautiful anger, and of a sense of wholeness. Part of wholeness is naming and claiming a sexual identity. What does it mean to belong to your sexual self? How do we authentically express our sexual desires and our unabashed ability to find pleasure in ourselves or with others?

Getting Curious

1.   Reflect on what it would look like to belong to yourself.

2.   What would it look like to belong to your sexual self?

3.   If you hadn't been shaped by sexual shame from purity culture, how would you connect with your body? Would you allow yourself to just be when you are sexually exploring?

4.   What would it mean to "rock the boat" as it relates to your sexuality?

Moving Forward in this Chapter

The remainder of this chapter is meant to give you some tangible ways to begin seeing your story and your experience of shame in a new light. We release shame by inhabiting the whole expression of our sexual being and by allowing ourselves to journey and to meet the intensity of the emotions we have connected to sex.

So, this is your time. As we move forward, I will offer you several more

"Getting Curious" questions and reflections. Give your sexuality a voice, share your stories, breathe into this acceptance and be aware as it moves through every part of your body.

Telling your story, sharing it fully with someone who will not respond in judgment is liberating. Shame gets worn out the more we speak the words it tells us to hide from the world. I can almost guarantee that if you start telling your own story (to a safe person), you will soon learn you are not alone. You will soon learn that your sexuality, wounds and all, connect you with others. We move beyond shame by using our voice, bringing to life what we want and don't want, our longings and desires, and by owning that we were designed for pleasure.

Embodiment

For various reasons many of us do not feel at home within our bodies. We are disconnected from our bodies – whether by trauma, objectification, sexism, sizeism – and with this disconnection comes the cost of living as a ghost; a phantom version of what we could truly be. Before we discuss embodiment, I want to address disembodiment and give you an example of how it can happen.

I was not expecting to have issues with food. In many ways, I hadn't given my body shape too much thought. Then, Covid happened. All of a sudden, I kept walking around my house thinking "I'm so fat." First, I am very aware that I am and likely will be to some extent fat phobic. Second, I have to work every single day to call myself on size-ist comments that are so automatic. And, during Covid, I decided one day that I would start counting calories. Mind you, I never thought of calories before this moment. I got an app and started messing around with the "perfect" number. Going to 1800, 1500, 1300, 1100 – trying to get the number smaller and smaller. I made a great little game out of how many "bonus" calories I could get in a day. I shared my numbers with my husband with so much pride and thought I really accomplished something . . . by ignoring my bodily cues... and I started to shrink.

As it shrunk, my body became a stranger to me. For example, I got this crazy rash that moved all over my body like it was something trying to claw its way out of me. I denied myself things I wanted (cake, a beer, pasta) every day. Coincidentally (or not), I started hating my life. I hated me, my husband, all the things I felt I had to do every day, such as parenting or exercise, all while trying to be "healthy" (aka, starve myself). My brain started to get fuzzy, and I was struggling to recall details in conversations. I was so weary all the time. Do you know those scenes in movies where the main character is walking in slow motion, but everything in the environment around them is moving so quickly? That's how I felt. I couldn't think. I couldn't move, and I couldn't feel. I was completely severed from myself. Our mind and our body are intimately connected, and when something isn't right with the body it can change the way we view ourself and the world. To survive this, we ignore what the body is trying to communicate.

I share all this to paint a picture of the opposite of embodiment. That was my story of disembodiment, and while I played a part in getting to that place, I also want us to be aware that disembodiment is also a result of patriarchy, racism, sexism, legalism, ableism, and the other systems of white supremacy that seek to divide and control us. We begin to see our body as a thing or object, something that does something for us – a tool to manipulate – rather than an embodied being or being present and available to your body. Hillary McBride is a psychologist and embodiment researcher, and in her recent book, *The Wisdom of Your Body*, she defines embodiment as the "practice of experiencing the body as a sensing, relating, rhythmic self (p.14)." She also says, "Embodiment is a kind of re-membering of who we really are...Embodiment is a coming home, a remembering of wholeness, and a reunion with the fullness of ourselves (p.14)."

When was the last time you felt home in your own body? When was the last time your body felt alive – like there was zest for life moving from your toes to fingertips. When was the last time you slowed and quieted your breath enough to feel your own heartbeat? When have you looked, truly looked at yourself, and thought, "I'm home."

I'd like to say that I am in a place where I look in the mirror each morning, put a hand over my heart and sigh, while saying, "I'm home," but I'm not there yet. I am working on letting different parts of my body touch at the same time, or buying clothes that fit my body and make it cozy rather than trying to manipulate my body and imprison it into too small leggings. I stopped running. I loved running, but then, I think it became warped in some way. It just became another tool to stop feeling. Now, my daughter tries to burrow into my soft stomach each night like it's her favorite pillow. She feels at home with my body. It is her home, and so, it becomes mine as well.

Embodiment is the opposite of what purity culture did to us. Purity culture ruptured the beautiful connection with which we came into the world. It told us not to feel sexual, or erotic, and to fall in line and submit. Submit to your husband. Submit to your pastor. Submit to your shitty manager or boss, because you are not your own – your body belongs to another. Embodiment is a key factor in sexual freedom (whatever this may look like for you). Embodied sexuality is something we were never told about in purity culture and, likely, something many of you haven't heard before. If we think about coming home with our sexuality or remembering the deep sense of peace when our bodies and minds are aware of one another, we might think of sexual embodiment as a full expression of our sexuality using our senses, fantasies, soul, minds, and sense of body.

When we are practicing embodied sexuality, we are our bodies during sexual exploration. We track and connect with sensations, feelings, and pleasure. We engage with what we are seeing, hearing, feeling and we move from our heads to below our necks. We leave the worry, self-evaluation, control, and fear, and we move into the present moment to tune into what our intuition, heart, and sexuality are experiencing. We have to move from doing to being. Let your sexual expressions be creative and reactive to the moment so you know what gives you pleasure and connection to yourself or a partner(s).

For example, to be embodied means that when you are triggered by a thought such as, "This is taking too long" or "I'm not turned on enough," and this occurs when you are IN THE MIDDLE of an erotic experience, you *resist* defensive strategies to move to your cognitions and begin evaluating. Instead, you drop into your body and breathe. Almost everything about sex also concerns the body, leading one to believe that sexuality is an innate part of embodiment. When you can focus on being embodied during a sexual experience, then the game completely changes! It may be something as small as slowing down a breath and then, suddenly feeling in tune with everything the body is experiencing. We notice the softness of our partner's skin, or even our own skin. We tune into the finger that runs down a spine or the curve of a breast and when we shiver in response, we breathe into that moment, that sensation.

Integrating embodiment practices is key in learning how to connect to your body and spirit. This may look like masturbation or self-pleasure, pleasure from any physical activity, movement, or breath work, and listening to your own internal reactions and then acting on those. Honestly, we just need to get into our bodies in whatever way feels most comfortable to us. We need our body, mind, and spirit to be congruent with one another. We need to let our awareness and emotions rise to the surface and be curious rather than silence ourselves. It is imperative that you, very gently, begin to explore and find a way to practice and experience pleasure in whatever capacity you are able to. Contrary to what we learned from purity culture, allowing ourselves pleasure is one of the most compassionate things we can do.

To do this, I will often use in therapy, a common technique called Sensate Focus, developed by Linda Weiner and Constance Avery-Clark (2017). It's a practice that focuses, first, on embodiment and connection with the self, and often, this will progress into sexual embodiment. Typically, this type of intervention is best done with a partner(s), but I have found that individuals can benefit from it as well. Sensate Focus is a series of structured touching and discovering. It's meant to explore your partner's body and your own body in a non-demanding and curious way. Non-demanding exploration involves touching, whether yourself or partner, for your own interest without focusing on pleasure, sexual response, or relaxation. Sensate Focus guides a person to center on texture (smooth/rough), temperature(warm/cool), and pressure (firm/soft). This model gives permission to be present, to be available, to connect with your body, and to allow an involuntary response (i.e., relaxation, arousal, pleasure) to occur. Often, when we are able to take the overactive mind out of a connection with one's own body, then our being can begin to respond in a natural manner.

Getting Curious

1.   What percentage of the time are you present during a sexual experience?

2.   If your mind wanders (disconnects from the body), where does it go? What is the function of that?

3.   What would embodied sexuality look like for you?

Self-Compassion

Purity culture messaging conveniently left out any path towards removing shame and reuniting with oneself. It's unsurprising, but still sad nonetheless. Coming out of purity culture and feeling potentially disconnected from your body and your sexuality can often create a lack of intimacy with oneself or with a partner, as well as a hopelessness that you will "never get it right." Imagine a person goes years with this narrative. What likely becomes commonplace is a deep sense of (false) blame as they tell themself it is their problem and if they could "just get it right," then sex would be easy. Beyond this, there are many other ways that sex could be tied to shame for a person. One person might have body shame, which makes them uncomfortable during sex or never wanting to be uncovered. Others may worry about their "performance" or being able to provide pleasure to their partner. People get embarrassed if they can't orgasm or can't help their partner reach orgasm. Often, there are multiple concerns happening at once, and it makes it seem that enjoying sex is impossible.

When we are drowning in shame or guilt, what we need most is compassion. For ourselves, past and present, we need kindness and self-compassion. Sometimes these terms can seem too abstract, so let me give you some more helpful, specific definitions. Self-compassion refers to a person's ability to be kind, loving, tolerant, forgiving, and generous towards oneself, especially when life events do not turn out the way we desire them to turn out (Neff, 2003, 2011). This type of compassion is a way of being that helps a person to be less critical and more accepting of themself, particularly during a time of difficulty. Self-compassion involves responding to our shortcomings with kindness, mindfulness, and an understanding that limitations or difficulties are a part of common humanity and that experiencing limitations can be what connects us to all others. We are all very ordinary human beings, and we can begin to love our ordinariness as a sacred expression of our own nobility, courage, and respect. Self-compassion involves three main components: (1) self-kindness, (2) mindfulness, and (3) common humanity (Neff, 2003). When we blend these components with sexuality, we have a path for how to move through some of the hang-ups that purity culture imposed upon us.

The first component of self-compassion is self-kindness. The first component of self-compassion is self-kindness. Rather than being judgmental of shortcomings and implementing self-punishing strategies for change, self-compassion leads individuals to consider their inadequacies with self-kindness, allowing for change unhindered by shame or guilt. Self-kindness can remind us that no one is perfect, and if we create a narrative that everyone but us has sex figured out, then we are just robbing ourselves of joy. When kindness is present, we can create separation from perceived failures from who we truly are and cultivate greater resilience. Self-kindness helps us to ally with ourselves by fostering an inner dialogue that is gentle and absent of judgment, criticism, and evaluation.

Real-life sex is far from perfect. There are ways our bodies can't move or bend. There are so many sounds, strappy things get stuck where they shouldn't, and self-kindness can help us to approach those moments with a sense of humor and playfulness by using the "imperfect" moments as opportunities for intimacy. When we can be vulnerable, knowing that we will address ourselves with kindness, it becomes easier to risk during sexual encounters. This may look like actually asking for what you want or need, letting go and losing yourself in a moment or sensation, and relishing the experience of giving and receiving pleasure. Yes, these are all typical and appropriate things to do. Purity culture told us we should feel guilty about our pleasure, and we do not have to believe this lie any longer.

The second component of self-compassion is mindfulness. In this context, mindfulness means present-moment awareness without any judgment or interpretation. In this way, we can be present with what we are noticing during a sexual encounter, especially one that we perceive as not going so well. We then approach our problems rather than avoiding thoughts and feelings because mindfulness teaches us to stop our avoidance strategies. When we are mindful, we refrain from negative evaluations during sex and, instead, practice curiosity or simply observation of the moment. For example, let's say a conflict or miscommunication occurs with a partner during a sexual moment. Being mindful allows a person to note differences (simply an observation) and to see them only as differences with a partner rather than to try to make an evaluation.

Let's say I approach a partner to initiate sex, and my partner says, "No." In this scenario, I might be thinking, "My partner doesn't want me. What's wrong with me?" A mindful approach, however, would mean noticing (observing) my emotional reactivity and, then, becoming curious in a non-judgmental, non-evaluative way. I might begin to wonder instead, why my partner is distracted or unable to engage in that moment. What is their deeper message to me that is hiding behind the "No?" Perhaps they are tired. Perhaps they are stressed about work. Perhaps they are struggling with their own body image issues. Important to notice, here, is that none of these observations have anything to do with me or with something being wrong with me. Instead, they may be opportunities for me to ask gentle questions of my partner, and in doing so, I transform my own shame of rejection into something beautiful and life-giving...reconnection with myself and with my partner.

The third component of self-compassion is what's known as remembering our common humanity. Once we can adopt self-kindness and attention to the present moment, we are able to view our personal failings or shortcomings as something common to all people. The suffering we experience is part of the greater human experience – an experience where there is suffering but also positive moments. When we are able to embrace common humanity, we can become more oriented to openness and connectedness with ourselves and others. This can be especially meaningful when we consider being open and connected with an intimate partner.

Self-compassion is imperative in decreasing shame around sexuality. It can help to remind us there is no "perfect" sexual situation. Pressuring yourself to be confident and all-knowing in the bedroom only adds to a sexual shame narrative (i.e., I'm not enough, I have to do more, what's wrong with me). Every time we connect sexually with ourselves or with another the encounter is different, making it incredibly difficult to have a concrete goal for how sex is "supposed" to be. Having this mindset where we have high expectations (and demands) for ourselves typically leads to disappointment. Every expectation, in fact, is a future disappointment waiting to happen. Instead, when we can keep an open mind, staying curious and utilizing self-compassion, what we end up with is more satisfying sexual experiences.

When we own our sexually imperfect selves and start to see our sexuality as evolving over the work of a lifetime, what we are really doing is creating a space for joy and connection to our sexual selves. When we can stay present in the moment, let go of expectations, and become interested in what this sexual encounter can help us learn about ourselves, we become aware of new ways of experiencing pleasure and decreasing sexual shame. A piece of this is truly showing up as ourselves by practicing self-kindness and authenticity. Then, our erotic confidence can increase, and we can begin to be seen more genuinely and fully as our whole self. Self-compassion in sexuality involves physical nakedness along with "emotional nakedness" – a willingness to be exposed, accessible and to allow care in a vulnerable space (Fraser et al., 2023). If none of what is said so far leads you to see self-compassion as necessary, then I am happy to tell you that orgasm is linked with self-compassion as relatively new research indicates that those who report greater self-compassion are likely to report greater orgasm consistency (Ferreira, Rigby, and Cobb, 2020).

Good Enough Sex (GES)

I do want to share something that, to me, is a wonderful example of the impact self-compassion can have on sexuality, and it's what is known as the "Good Enough Sex" (GES) model by Metz and McCarthy (2007). I like this model because the creators talk about real sex in everyday relationships. The model helps to balance the unrealistic expectations we often have about sex and factors in the impact that cessation of the limerence (or honeymoon) stage has on a relationship. It is fairly true, for example, that about 6-24 months after the start of a sexual relationship, there is a shift where we often see spontaneity, excitement, and novelty fade from sexual encounters. The GES model is a couple concept rather than individual performance, and it emphasizes variable and flexible sexual response rather than demanding performance perfection.

There are 12 points to the GES model (italicized comments are from McCarthy and McCarthy, 2019):

1. Sex is a positive dimension in life, an invaluable part of your individual and couple comfort, intimacy, desire, pleasure, eroticism, and satisfaction.

- *The key for desire is positive anticipation, feeling you deserve sexual pleasure, freedom and choice regarding sexual scenarios and techniques, and the unpredictability of the sexual experience.*
- *Eroticism involves mystery, creativity, risk-taking, experimentation, etc.*

2. Relationship and sexual satisfaction are the ultimate focus and are essentially intertwined. You are an "intimate sexual team."

- *Viewing your partner as being your erotic and intimate ally and adopting positive, realistic expectations.*

3. Realistic psychological, biological, and relational expectations are essential for sexual satisfaction.

- *The core of eroticism is intense sexual feelings or sensations. It involves manual, oral, rubbing, and vibrator stimulation in addition to intercourse. It involves 6-10 sensations and can be enjoyed without intercourse.*
- *Desire is facilitated by receptivity and responsivity to giving and receiving pleasure-oriented touch.*
- *Non-demand pleasuring includes affectionate, sensual, and playful touch. Pleasure has value whether or not it transitions to arousal.*
- *Most sex is asynchronous (meaning both partners may not climax or experience the same levels of pleasure) yet positive.*

4. Good physical health and healthy behavioral habits are vital for sexual health. You value your sexual body and your partner's sexual body.

- *Desire is promoted by a healthy body, good behavioral habits – sleep, accepting changes with aging, and maintaining a self-accepting body-image.*

5. Relaxation is the foundation for sexual pleasure and response.

- *If a person is not able to be present, is anxious, or in fight-or-flight, desired sexual response will not likely occur.*

6. Desire and satisfaction are more important than arousal and orgasms.

- *Satisfaction involves feeling good about yourself as a sexual person and energized as a sexual couple.*
- *The key to satisfaction is positive realistic expectations.*

7. Valuing variable, flexible couple sexual experiences and abandoning the "need" for perfect individual sex performance inoculates you against sexual dysfunction by overcoming performance pressures, fears of failure, and partner rejection.

- *What is best is to be able to turn toward one another whether sex was dynamite, very good, good, okay, mediocre, dissatisfying, or dysfunctional. Remember – intimate sexual team in good and bad times.*

8. The five purposes for sex (pleasure, intimacy, tension reduction, self-esteem, reproduction) are integrated into your sexual relationship.

· *Sex has multiple purposes. It is advantageous to communicate with your partner about what the purpose is for you and your partner.*

9. Integrate and flexibly use the three sexual arousal styles (partner interaction, self-entrancement, role enactment).

· *Partner interaction = arousal or eroticism which features each partner's arousal enhancing the others.*
· *Self-entrancement = taking turns with one partner the giver the other the receiver. The receiving partner's responsibility enhances your sexual experience.*
· *Role enactment = using outside resources to provide an erotic charge (sex toys, playing out fantasies, blindfolds/handcuffs, stripping for your partner, etc.)*

10. Gender differences are respectfully valued, and similarities mutually accepted.

· *For couples under 40, sex is better for men. For couples over 60, sex is better for women. It is less complex for a penis owner to orgasm compared to a vulva owner.*

11. Sex is integrated into real life and real life is integrated into sex. Sexuality is developing, growing and evolving throughout your life.

· *The ability to be sexual, to be present, to desire your partner can be impacted by the tasks or the day, stress, or whether you feel emotionally connected or not.*

12. Sexuality is personalized: Sex can be playful, energizing, spiritual, special.

· *You/your partner(s) get to shape a sexual connection that is unique to your relationship.*

Overall, this model really just encourages a person/couple to explore what is positive and meaningful in intimacy. In the GES model, the ultimate focus is intimacy, with a high value on connection, pleasure, and mutuality. There is a vast amount of research and writing done on the GES model, and I encourage you to seek out this information and apply it to your sexual relationship. This model is highly valued and used often in couples sex therapy because it promotes the idea that there are multiple dimensions of sex, such as to learn to have play, openness, and have your expectations be reality-based. Remember that the striving is not for perfection or orgasm, and the most important piece is the ability to turn towards your partner when sex isn't as you expected rather than to collapse with shame. Sadly, self-compassion is often not the first thing that comes to mind when we think of good sex. So often, individuals or couples can put pressure on themselves or have unrealistic expectations about what sex will be like or "should" be like. This lacks self-kindness, an understanding that everyone has sex that is fantastic or mediocre or dysfunctional, and that there is benefit to being a sexual ally with yourself and your partner.

Getting Curious

1. How would you currently assess your relationship with self-compassion?

2. Where do you know the presence of lack of self-kindness, mindfulness, and seeing suffering as a connection to common humanity?

3. If you are finding it difficult to identify where you may be with self-compassion, then consider taking the self-compassion survey found at: https://self-compassion.org/self-compassion-test/

Re-Authoring Your Sexual Narrative

Your sexual narrative has the ability to create a story about what sex is or is not, what constitutes pleasure, and what is sexually unacceptable. You may have spent the entirety of your sexual experiences thinking you are broken because you can't orgasm, because your sex drive is lower than your partner's, or because you can't stand to touch parts of your own body. The truth is that we often tell ourselves we are broken rather than examining how we hold onto a broken narrative, a falsehood about who and what we are "supposed to" be as sexual creatures. All of us have stories that are problematic, especially as it relates to the interplay of sexuality and religion, and to move towards healing, we have to begin to unpack and work through these narratives. Doing so has the ability to seize the sexual autonomy that you already possess but maybe haven't tapped into.

Each sexual narrative is unique and is constructed from a personal history, culture, the relationships you've had, and the family they grew up in. Narratives are shaped by hope and dreams just as much as they are shaped by disappointment and wounds. I love how Suzaane Iasenza (2020) describes how narratives first begin. She writes, "One's earliest narratives of sexuality develop long before learned language...One's first experiences as an infant consist of physical sensation and pleasure. The skin tingles with touch, tiny ears soak up comforting murmurs and heartbeats; the tongue experiences the sweet delights of flavor" (p.4). Our story begins the minute we take our first breath and feel ourselves fill us with life.

As life continues, our narratives become twisted as we learn that bodily pleasure (or touch) is no longer permissible. We lose the intimacy we needed to survive as infants and are told touch is wrong and only allowed in certain contexts. We lose our sense of what provides pleasure, and we use our religion and society to craft new narratives about pleasure, intimacy, love, and sin. We want deep committed relationships but are unable to risk the vulnerability needed to give birth to those dynamics. We begin to shame ourselves for times we become aroused when we are "not supposed to" or to reject ourselves when we are not aroused by what is "supposed to" turn us on. In addition to these stories, we also sometimes hear other stories – contradictory ones – and the narratives we craft become complex as life teaches us that sexuality is multilayered and incredibly fluid. We learn that gender is not fixed, our sexual preferences change, that we can be madly in love with a person and not have sexual desire towards them.

Much like you were able to explore your sexual script earlier in this book, it is also imperative that you examine your sexual narrative and begin to re-author your story. Seeing yourself and your history in a new light can increase empathy for yourself and also re-orient you to a sexuality that is authentic and true for you. In this section, I hope to offer a few ways for you to really dig into your story and see what needs to be tossed out, replanted, or is longing for watering and sunlight.

First, I invite you to take a broad look at your life and identify what experiences or parts have contributed to your current narrative. This can be as simple as a bullet-point list and include things such as "playing doctor" as a child, being the victim of sexual abuse, your parents' relational dynamic, pornography you found/viewed in your life, and dating or close relationships. Start at your earliest memories and work forward. After you've completed this list, go back to the beginning and try to summarize the meaning taken from that event. For example, let's say you observed your parents' dynamic as an angry mother and a subservient father, and you recalled a horrific fight you witnessed. You became so terrified but were fearful of your mom directing her anger towards you, so you stayed silent and tried not to feel the fear, thinking it would only make things worse. The meaning that you might identify is that "it is too unsafe to share my true feelings, especially when it comes to fear." This could impact sexuality in that it hinders you from being truly vulnerable or communicative about intimacy and desire, and you struggle to challenge the belief that your shared emotions will be seen as a burden. Taking a broad outlook and zooming back in on meaning-making can be extremely beneficial in that it allows you to see pieces of your life that are directly connected to sexuality, intimacy, and desire. Then, we have the opportunity to stop personalizing sexual difficulties or shame as "my fault" and to understand how so many aspects of life contribute to the current sexual experiences one is having.

Another area for exploration is identifying what model of sexuality you are using to determine your own sexual functioning. One of the first models of sexuality was identified in 1966 by William Master and Virginia Johnson and was known as the "Human Sexual Response Cycle" (see Figure 1). At the time (and for decades after) most people, researchers, and clinicians viewed this as the gold standard for understanding the human sexual response pattern. It has four stages and is linear, meaning that the phases were successive. The four stages are: (1) excitement, (2) plateau, (3) orgasm, and (4) resolution. This looks like what we often see in the media and became the expectation for many people from which to model an understanding of sex.

Figure 1

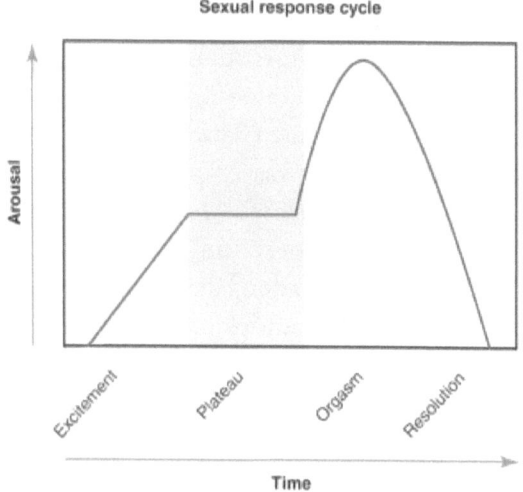

Fig. 1. Masters-Johnson Model of sexual response. Adapted from Masters WH JV. Human Sexual Response. Little, Brown & Co, 1966.

In the excitement phase there is sexual arousal (often portrayed as spontaneous), and it's marked by increased heart rate, respiration, vasocongestion (this is where blood vessels engorge), and a penile erection can occur. A hardening of the nipples and vaginal lubrication also occurs during this phase. The plateau phase is an intensification of the first. Here, you might see increased blood flow, heavier, more rapid breathing, muscle tension, the clitoris becomes more sensitive, and we see pre-seminal fluid secreted at the penile opening (what most people call precum).

In the orgasm phase – well – orgasm occurs. It's seen as the peak or climax of excitement. It may be helpful to know that not all people easily or ever reach this phase. It's characterized by involuntary muscle contractions throughout the body, and it is normally paired with a euphoric feeling or tension release. This phase is where all the tension that was built in the first two phases is released and ejaculation happens. In the resolution phase, the body returns to baseline, and all parts of your body and bodily function return to a pre-arousal state. Over time, this model came under criticism and was seen as too narrow and male-based due to its focus on sexual response as spontaneous and linear. Criticism also suggested that there was a heavy focus on physiological response while leaving out the emotional and contextual aspects of sexual response (Rowland and Gutieerez, 2017).

Another model of sexuality was created by Helen Kaplan in 1979 and was known as having three phases: (1) desire, (2) excitement, and (3) orgasm. What was considered novel and a contribution to the field of human sexuality was that Kaplan added desire as a part of sexual response. Kaplan viewed desire as a prerequisite for excitement and arousal, and therefore, this model continued with the view that sexual response was linear. Kaplan's phase of desire took into account that a body needs to be physiologically aroused. Despite the linearity of the model, the desire phase was an attempt to account for emotional aspects, the need for subjective enjoyment, and a motivation to seek out and respond to sexual stimulation (Rowland and Gutieerez, 2017). A note about spontaneous desire (as it was present in both the Masters and Johnson and Kaplan models of sexual response) is that a belief in spontaneous desire can often be a setup for most people. It's problematic because it sets both women and men up to believe women should have the ability to be spontaneously turned on and ready for sex at a moment's notice, which simply isn't true for many women. These early models also led to many women being labeled as having a sexual dysfunction rather than having reality taken into account (i.e., women typically need to be aroused before a desire happens).

More recently, a model focusing on women's sexual responses was created by Rosemary Basson (2001; 2005) who hypothesized that the human sexual response is circular rather than linear. Her model (see Figure 2) incorporated the need for emotional intimacy and satisfaction since it considers relationship factors as having the ability to impact sexual response negatively or positively. Her model takes into account that desire can be spontaneous or responsive (desire builds or shows up after an attempt to arouse has begun), and it suggests that orgasms do not need to be present to experience sexual satisfaction.

Figure 2

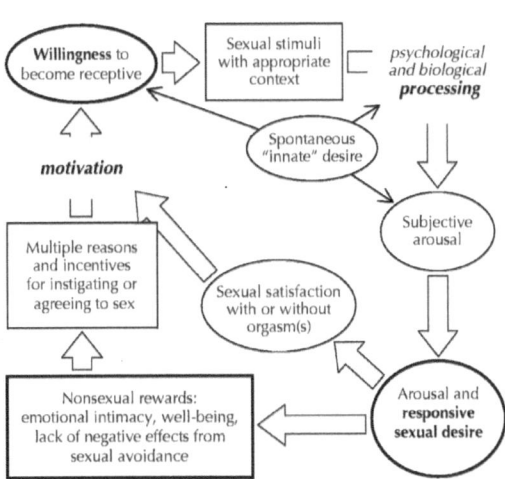

Figure 2: Sexual response cycle showing responsive desire during the sexual experience along with spontaneous desire (Basson, 2005. Modified from Basson 2001).

To me, this model is the friendliest and most realistic model of sexual response for several reasons. The first is that it takes into account how real-life impacts functioning in that sometimes where we need to start is at *willingness* to be sexual rather than feeling sexual desire or arousal. Second, this model highlights that appropriate context is needed to get to arousal. This means that it is likely extremely difficult to become aroused if your mind is on the dirty dishes, how a business meeting went haywire earlier in the day, or how you feel emotionally disconnected from your partner. And, finally, this model captures how many individuals enter a sexual encounter with no desire and, instead, enter with a willingness to be intimate with a trust that desire will follow. This is referred to as responsive desire – the willingness to enter a sexual encounter, being stimulated, and becoming aroused as a "response" to the engagement with sexual stimuli.

In Figure 2, you can see the "initial" stage (on the left) where the person is sexually neutral but has positive motivation. Some motivations might be wanting to express love, to give and receive physical pleasure, to increase emotional closeness, and to increase a sense of wellbeing. These motivations can lead to a willingness to become sexually active by consciously focusing on sexual stimuli. The stimuli is then processed cognitively and influenced by biological and psychological factors. This processing results in a subjective sexual arousal. With continued stimulation, sexual pleasure/excitement becomes more intense, which triggers a desire for sex. Sexual satisfaction (regardless of the presence of orgasm or not) results when a woman is stimulated long enough, is focused, enjoys the sensation of sexual arousal, and experiences positive outcomes from the experience (Basson, 2005).

The main reason for being able to assess which model of sexual response you've ascribed to is that, whether you realize it or not, you've likely internalized an idea of how you are meeting or not meeting what you think of as "normal" sexual functioning. I would encourage you to begin to view your past sexual experiences and expectations through the lens of the Basson model where there is flexibility and freedom. Begin to consider, for example, how acceptance of responsive desire and letting go of a belief that you are to have spontaneous desire may change things for you.

The next component in re-authoring your sexual narrative is to really lean into this idea of sexual freedom. Look back at the past with the mindset that each consensual encounter, fantasy, or sexual thought was allowable. Look back knowing that you had freedom and permission to experience those moments, and that shame was never tied to sexuality. How does that change the view of your current sexuality and sexual desires?

A final piece in re-authoring is looking to the present and the future and being flexible and open with what might contribute to sexual connection with yourself and/or a partner and build a sexual menu. A sexual menu consists of what a person wants or imagines could increase a sense of eroticism and sexuality. This could be something body-based, including sex or masturbation, but it could also include anything connected to pleasure – a meal you've been longing to savor, a sunrise, feeling connected with nature. Making a menu can help you shift how you see yourself – from someone who feels that they "have" to experience shame when sexual to someone who is aware that sexuality is a part of who they are and can be embodied in any manner that fits for you.

Getting Curious

1. Begin the process of re-authoring your sexual narrative. It is helpful to first identify the stories you have been telling yourself about your sexuality and then identify the narrative you want to move towards.

2. Oftentimes this is helpful to do with a therapist, but if that is not available to you, then try to start on your own.

Spiritual Practices for Sexual Wholeness

Perhaps spiritual practices and sexuality feel like they are at opposite ends of the spectrum. This is likely due to purity culture's ability to connect sexuality with shame rather than to see sexuality as something sacred. My personal ability to view the relationship between sex and spirituality differently has changed quite drastically over time, for multiple reasons. One reason is due to the research that came from Chuck MacKnee (2002), which I'll attempt to summarize for you. Dr. MacKnee did a qualitative study of ten individuals in which he wanted to "develop thematic descriptions of meaningful experiences that were simultaneously sexual and spiritual from a Christian perspective" (p.235). Specifically, participants in his study self-identified as someone who was part of a profound event where sexual and spiritual connection occurred (e.g., a person is praying, feeling God speak to them, and engaged in sex with a partner simultaneously). From his interviews, he found twelve themes that emerged regarding the meaning and experience of sexual and spiritual encounters.

The themes his research identified included: a sense of wonder and awe, emotional cleansing, the felt presence of God, an intense union, euphoria, intense physical arousal, transcendence, holistic involvement (spirit, body, mind), a sense of being blessed and gifted, ineffable mystery, and a sense of sacredness and worship. Dr. MacKnee's research also explored themes of the "after effects" of these encounters, which included: transformation and healing, empowerment and purpose, passionate awareness and connection, affirmation of Godly beliefs, gratefulness, and a sense of gender equality. One of the things I love most in his research is that all these experiences happen without plan or with these effects in the minds of the participants. God just showed up in these encounters and changed lives. Dr. MacKnee suggests, "If God's passion created human passion, human desire can be understood as a relentless returning to that place where all things are one" (p. 242).

When I consider what sort of spiritual practice can be drawn from this research, I imagine the practice of openness and freedom. If we can think of sexuality as something where our passion comes to life, then we can take a more open stance to the place our desire leads us. We can begin to actively view sex as something where our hunger for a deep and joyous connection with our own bodies and the body of our partner mirrors how God desperately pursues us. Are we, then, being "Christ-like" when we yearn for our body to connect with another, to get lost in pleasure, to seek oneness? This is a major shift in perspective for many who grew up within purity culture, and it is truly transformative for one's spiritual life.

Another practice that can lead us towards sexual wholeness is a willingness to let go. It takes effort and intentionality to step back and start examining all the "truths" about sex you learned in your past. Give yourself permission to let go, and look for the alternative! Be willing to see new insights in Christian teachings that affirm sexual diversity. For instance, what would it be like to look at the story of David and Jonathan and see them as lovers? The Bible says David's love for Jonathan was more than that of a woman's – there was a reason that was recorded in Holy Scripture.

Another practice might be a new openness to interpretation. The academic word for this is hermeneutics, but in terms of spiritual practice, one expression of this is *Lectio Divina* where the reader meditates, or prays, over a particular passage multiple times while allowing the text to speak to them in new ways. What if, for example, we get curious about why the Bible states that God created humans in God's image, in the image of God (s)he created him (Adam), male and female. In Hebrew, "Adam" is not a proper name. It simply means "humanity." All of humanity and all of Creation is created in God's image.

We've ignored this passage for so long, but put into context of the Creation story, we can see that God laid out multiple binaries in addition to male and female (night and day, light and dark). At first glance, these look like rather strict binaries, but with some openness, we could see them as an indication of the existence of spectrums. In the New Testament, Paul actually asks us to do this when he teaches us that there are no more binaries – there is no more male nor female, Jew nor Gentile – because all are one within the Body of Christ, a holistic spectrum of unity in diversity. In terms of spiritual practice, this is often referred to as non-dualistic thinking. Let's take "day and night" and apply this logic. In between light and dark we have twilight, a sunrise, a sunset, dusk – multiple ways to see what exists beyond just light and dark. Taking this approach, it isn't too far-fetched to believe that God possesses all genders (and no genders). Ethiopian eunuchs, for example, possess no gender or sexual organs, and they are seen throughout scripture as "set apart" ("holy") for various purposes. We could wonder why one of the first confirmed baptisms was of an Ethiopian eunuch – a person whose sexuality was expressed in a manner considered quite out of the norm in its time.

Also, we can't forget the classic – Song of Solomon. This entire set of scriptures lays out an erotic, sensual interplay between two unmarried individuals. They are both clear about their desires and passions for one another – both the male and the female in the passages express desire. And, while the biblical sexting is happening, no one is mentioning marriage or pregnancy – this was all purely for pleasure.

Another practice I would invite you into is to engage in the uncovering of your own sexuality. In spiritual practice terms, we might refer to this as a process of clarification – a way of seeing more clearly our own bodies and the world around us. To begin to see your body as something passionate and capable of ecstasy is quite empowering. One of the very first steps in this uncovering process is to learn about your own body. Doing this can help invite a sense of safety in learning how your body responds. I'd like us to get familiar with all of the parts. Figure 3 is a (crude) drawing of my own that shows what it would look like if a person with a vulva was lying down on their back and we were facing their genitals. The vulva is the part of female genitals located on the outside of the body. It includes the labia, clitoris, vaginal opening, and the opening to the urethra (the hole where urine comes out of). Most people call all of this the "vagina," but what they are actually talking about is the vulva. Vagina is only one part of the vulva (the vagina is where a penis would enter or where a child is birthed from).

Figure 3

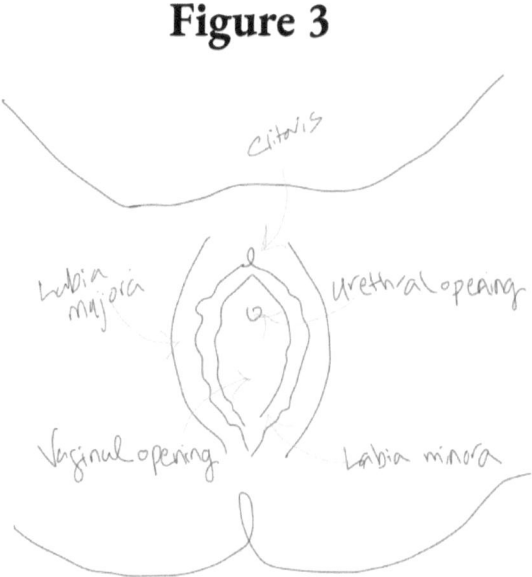

Figure 3: Picture of a vulva if someone were lying down.

So, the first thing we want to look at is identifying the clitoris, otherwise known as the glans. It is located at the top of the vulva where the inner lips meet. Everyone's clitoral size is different and can vary from the size of a small pea to as big as a thumb. The tip of the clitoris is covered by the clitoral hood. When a person with a vulva becomes aroused the clitoral hood pulls back and the clitoris can become more prominent and erect. We've already covered that the urethra opening is where urine exits the body. The labia, consisting of the inner (minora) and outer (majora), are the folds of skin that are around the opening of the vagina. Sometimes these are referred to as "lips." The outer lips are typically fleshy and have pubic hair on them while the inner lips are inside your outer lips and are void of pubic hair. The labia extends from the clitoris to beneath the vagina. It's important to note that labias can all look quite different. They can be short, long, wrinkled, or smooth. One lip may be longer than the other, and the color of the labia varies (from pink to brownish black) and can change color as a person ages. Both lips are sensitive, and when a person is aroused, the lips can swell.

I think one of the most convincing things for me that God is pro-pleasure is the clitoris, which leads me to a final and highly significant spiritual practice – pleasure. Figure 4 shows the anatomy of the clitoris. That tiny nub of flesh is only a small piece of the entire clitoris, which is mostly unseen. The unseen portion extends inside the body, back and down both sides of the vagina. This part is called the bulbs (roots) and crus (legs) and is about five inches long. It consists of a network of erectile tissue and nerves. When stimulated, a person can start to feel sexually aroused, feelings of sexual tension are heightened and often orgasm can occur. Whether or not a person has an orgasm, the sensation of the clitoris being stimulated typically feels good. The clitoris has over 10,000 nerve endings that work together to form intense pleasure whereas the penis has only about 4,000 nerve endings.

The clitoris is made up of spongy tissue that can become swollen when aroused. With its 10,000 nerve endings, it's clear the only function of the clitoris is pleasure. However, both the clitoris and the penis function correspondingly as sensory organs. They are both sensitive to touch and arousal. Both also have the ability to lead to orgasm. Moreover, both the clitoris and the penis have similar regions. Looking at Figure 5, we can see that the head of the penis (labeled as glans) is similar to the visible head of the clitoris. However, the rest of the clitoris is inside the body and unseen, whereas the head and shaft (the rest of the visible penis) are external to the body.

As mentioned earlier, the clitoris has a hood, which is pulled back when aroused to allow for maximum exposure and pleasure. The foreskin of a penis is similarly related (a foreskin is present when a penis is uncircumcised) in that if you pull the foreskin back, it will reveal the head/glans of the penis. It is important to remember that the head of the clitoris can greatly vary in size just as a penis (from glans to crus) can vary.

When education and empowerment is absent, the clitoris can often go unnoticed, which is detrimental for a sexual relationship. A recent study showed that only 18% of vulva owners can have an orgasm just by having penetrative sex (Herbenick, 2017). This means that about 80% of vulva owners need attention paid to the clitoris in order to achieve orgasm or increase chances of orgasm. I've met more than a few who have not had an orgasm (for many reasons), and one of the reasons for this is lack of awareness of or ability to tolerate having a clitoris. Some people don't want theirs touched because the vulva seems unfamiliar, or the sensation feels too out of control. Some are not used to the sensation of pleasure or arousal and become anxious. Others don't know how to touch themselves or communicate to a partner what touch is desired. Knowing about the clitoris and its sole purpose as a pleasure point is a spiritual insight in that we receive the gift and message that God designed us to experience pleasure. It is also important for us, especially those who grew up in purity culture, to know that a spiritual practice of pleasure is a right and good thing and that this pleasure can bring a desire to worship – whether worship of the Creator, of the ability for pleasure, or the wonder of one's own body. Indeed, anatomy really speaks to how humans are wired for pleasure.

Figure 4

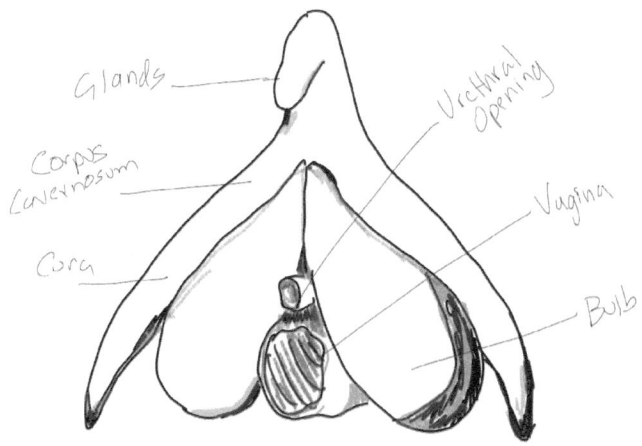

Figure 4: Anatomy of the clitoris

Figure 5

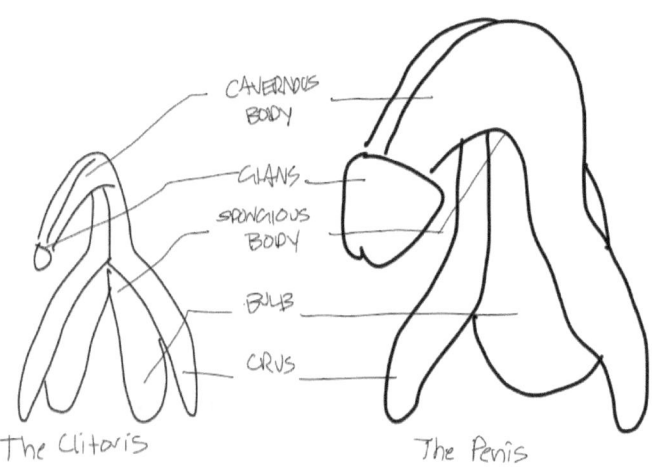

Figure 5: Anatomy of the penis and clitoris

Education and empowerment also reveals to us that we are more gender fluid than we often realize. For the first six weeks in the womb, interestingly, all fetuses are female. We all start our development journey with a clitoris. It is only 6-7 weeks into gestation when specific hormones may be released that creates changes resulting in the clitoris beginning to grow into a penis (Wizemann and Purdue, 2001). If testosterone is not present, then the tissue will develop into a vulva. In the womb, the male scrotum (testes) originally starts out as the outer labia. In males, the outer labia is fused together to make scrotum to hold the testicles. Whereas in a female fetus, the opening between the "lips" will remain present and begin to fill with the spongy tissue forming the labia majora. The bulb of the penis is a bundle of tissues that forms the visible ridge you can see at the bottom of the shaft. This correlates with the clitoral bulb. These structures extend inside the body on the inside edge of the crus of the clitoris. The bulbs can become engorged with blood when sexually aroused.

What a win for vulva owners – every fetus begins as female. Every being from its conception was made to experience intense pleasure. I see this as a clear message from the Creator. We were formed to experience pleasure. We were made for it.

Get Curious

1. What are some signs in your life that perhaps you were made to experience pleasure?

2. If you have not done this before, get yourself a handheld mirror and use it to see what your vulva looks like. Look for some of the parts mentioned in this chapter. Notice what it feels like, what color it is, the shape that makes it yours.

3. If you are curious about how unique each vulva can look, visit the labia library online.

Chapter Three References

Basson, R. (2001). Human sex-response cycles. *Journal of Sex & Marital Therapy*, 27, 33–43.

Basson, R. (2005). Women's sexual dysfunction: revised and expanded definitions. *Canadian Medical Association Journal*, 172(1), p.1328. doi: 10.1503/cmaj.1020174.

Brown, B. (2010). *Gifts of imperfection*. Hazelden Information & Educational Services.

McBride, H. (2021). *The wisdom of your body*. Harper Collins.

Ferreira, J. S., Rigby, R. A., & Cobb, R. J. (2020). Self-compassion moderates associations between distress about sexual problems and sexual satisfaction in a daily diary study of married couples. *Canadian. Journal of Human Sexuality*, 29 182–196. 10.3138/cjhs.2020-0009.

Fraser, A. M., Leavitt, C. E., Yorgason, J. B., & Price, A. A. (2023). "Feeling It": links between elements of compassion and sexual well-being. *Frontiers in Psychology*, 13. doi: 10.3389/fpsyg.2022.1017384.

Herbenick, D., Fu, T. C. (Jane)., Arter, J., Sanders, S., & Dodge, B. (2018). Women's experiences with genital touching, sexual pleasure, and orgasm: results from a U.S. probability sample of women ages 18 to 94. *Journal of Sex & Marital Therapy*, 44(2), 201-212, doi: **10.1080/0092623X.2017.1346530.**

Kaplan, H. S. (1979). *Disorders of sexual desire and other new concepts and techniques in sex therapy*. Brunner/Mazel Publications.

Macknee, C. M. (2002). Profound sexual and spiritual encounters among practicing Christians: a phenomenological analysis. *Journal of Psychology and Theology*, 30(3), 234–244. doi: **10.1177/009164710203000306.**

Masters, W. & Johnson, V. (1966). *Human sexual response*. Little, Brown.

McCarthy, B. & McCarthy, E. (2019). *Enhancing couple sexuality:*

Creating an intimate and erotic bond (1st ed.). Routledge. doi: 10.4324/9780429446092.

Metz, M. E. & McCarthy, B. W. (2007) The "Good-Enough Sex" model for couple sexual satisfaction. *Sexual and Relationship Therapy*, 22(3), 351-362, doi: 10.1080/14681990601013492.

Neff, K. D. (2003) Self-compassion: an alternative conceptualization of a healthy attitude toward oneself. *Self and Identity*, 2, 85-101. doi: 10.1080/15298860309032.

Neff, K. D. (2011). Self-compassion, self-esteem, and well-being. *Social and Personality Psychology Compass*, 5, 1-12. doi: 10.1111/j.1751-9004.2010.00330.x.

Rowland, D. & Gutierrez, B. (Eds.) (2017). *The SAGE encyclopedia of abnormal and clinical psychology.* (Vols. 1-7). SAGE Publications, Inc. doi: 10.4135/9781483365817.

Wizemann, T. M. & Pardue, M. L. (Eds.) (2001). Exploring the biological contributions to human health: does sex matter? *Institute of Medicine (US) Committee on Understanding the Biology of Sex and Gender Differences.* Washington (DC): National Academies Press. Committee on understanding the biology of sex and gender differences. Available from: https://www.ncbi.nlm.nih.gov/books/NBK222293/.

Chapter Four

Rebirthing Curiosity

This chapter is the one I've been looking forward to writing the most. It just feels like the "fun" chapter. One of the reasons I am so excited about it is that it invites us to view sexuality from multiple perspectives and angles. I take no stance that any one perception is the "right" or "wrong" perception, but I do enjoy being curious about what else there is for us. We know that sexuality is shaped by multiple factors, one of which is religious teaching and interpretations about what is allowed and what is "sin" when it comes to sexuality. It is for that reason that I find it meaningful to take another look.

In addition, I've spent numerous hours listening to the pain of people's stifled sexuality, the belief that who they are and how they show up is fundamentally wrong, and feeling so othered that they believe they will never belong. The truth is that if we only look at sexuality through one lens, then we shut down our own expression of creativity and zest. The following sections, then, will look at some "hot button issues" related to sexuality and the religious messaging that is accompanied by these expressions. I want to let you know that I am not sure where I land on all of these sexual expressions, but I am curious about what is hidden behind religious teaching. I am also curious about what we can learn about ourselves and our sexuality.

Getting Curious

1.   Write down what thoughts or values you hold about the following subjects:

     •   Masturbation
     •   Sexually explicit materials
     •   Kink
     •   Consensual non-monogamy
     •   Gender identity
     •   Sexual orientation

The Narratives and a New View

Masturbation

Historically, most religions agreed that masturbation is spiritually and physically harmful. Take, for instance, John Wesley (founder of Methodism) who often preached that masturbation caused madness or a mental disorder. Ellen White (founder of Seventh Day Adventism) taught that masturbation was a vice (or sin) and had visions of disfigured humans and the destruction of life due to masturbation (Numbers, 2003). The Catholic Church chastises masturbation as "an intrinsically gravely and disordered action" (Catholic Church, 2000, section 2352). Jehovah's Witnesses liken masturbation to a "form of uncleanness" that can cause mental corruption. Sexual self-pleasure is strictly forbidden by Mormons, Jains, Sikhs, Orthodox Jews, Buddhist Monks, and most facets of Islam.

I want to mention a particularly prominent American who was known for many interesting things (you should look up the enema yogurt combo he invented), one of them being his vocal anti-masturbation stance. His name was John Harvey Kellogg (as in the cereal). He held views that sex (including masturbation) was incredibly damaging to a person's health. In fact, it is said that he abstained from sex and never consummated his marriage. In 1877 he wrote, *Plain Facts for Old and Young: Embracing the Natural History and Hygiene of Organic Life*. In this work, Dr. Kellogg cataloged 39 different symptoms that were likely to affect a chronic masturbator, including defective development, mood swings, general infirmity, bashfulness, boldness, poor posture, painful joints, pickiness, acne, a desire for spicy foods, heart palpitations, and seizures. His solution for masturbation urges was a healthy diet. His theory was that bland, plain foods would curb sexual desires, which resulted in his invention of Kellogg's Corn Flakes. It is worth noting that in 1829 Sylvester Graham (a minister) invented the graham cracker to decrease the desire for "self-abuse" (i.e., masturbation) by males (Shryock, 1931). It wasn't until the birth of scientific sexuality research (Kinsey, Pomeroy, & Martin, 1948:1953), coupled with the sexual revolution of the 1960s, that social attitudes about masturbation shifted to one of acceptance.

Masturbation falls within the proverbial gray area of Christian sexual ethics. Like myself, you may be a person who thought for some time that masturbation was wrong, and you were told that it was a sin. I'm guessing that there was a particular part of scripture that was used to "prove" that masturbation is wrong. Was it the one about Onan in Genesis 38? I'll note that this story was actually about Tamar, but of course, the focus became the "male character." In this story, Onan was told by his dad Judah (and by God) that he needed to have intercourse with Tamar (the wife of his late brother) as Hebrew law commanded. The hope of this union was to procreate and raise offspring for his late brother. When Onan went to have sex with Tamar, he decided to "pull out" and "spilled his seed upon the ground." After this, God struck Onan dead.

The story is often told as a message about masturbation – that "spilling seed" is a sin and one that God punishes. However, there isn't any mention of masturbation. Instead, the sin was one of disregard for Hebrew law, God's direction, and a father's request. The "sin of Onan" refers to Onan's disregard for cultural norms and expectations, not to mention a direct command from God. If anything, this story is about a lack of surrender to God's will in favor of pursuing one's own self-interest, which is a highly relevant issue for our culture today. A more modern Christian view of this story recognizes that the spilling of seed in the story refers to coitus interruptus and not masturbation.

Another biblical passage often used in the denunciation of masturbation can be found in Matthew 5:27-30, which teaches Christians not to commit adultery, even in their heart. It is also the famous passage that instructs folks to cut off body parts that cause them to sin. The interpretation of this passage leading to the restrictive stance against masturbation typically looks like this: 1) Jesus condemns lust, 2) a person cannot masturbate without lusting, 3) thus, masturbation is absolutely a sin. However, I am not convinced that lust and the sexual desire, or arousal, that motivates masturbation are the same. This interpretation assumes that any masturbation stems from lust and is an example of absolutist thinking, which some Christians typically use when trying to avoid using logic and reason to employ moral discernment (Kwee and Hoover, 2008).

On the other hand, if one approaches this passage with a more discerning interpretation, then they might stumble into the idea that masturbation isn't categorically lustful; rather there is room to consider the context and intention of the engaged person. There are differences of intention that exist. One example of this difference in intention is the moral difference between masturbation done in the presence of an nonconsenting partner and masturbation done as sexual expression of the desire for connectedness to oneself or another. Indeed, Kwee and Hoover (2008) suggest that those who interpret Matthew 5:27-30 as condemning masturbation are missing the main thrust of Christ's teaching, which, when viewed in the context of the overall message and reason for Christ's ministry, is to free people from the condemnation of religious laws and teachings.

So, what if for hundreds of years, Christians have actually missed out on the benefits of masturbation? Benefits that occur on multiple levels. One of the first main benefits of masturbation is sexual pleasure. This may also be part of marital satisfaction. Some couples want to masturbate together (mutual masturbation). There can be pleasure from watching a partner masturbate. There can be flexibility in the frequency of sex in a marriage when masturbation is considered for one or the other partner. There can be a sense of empowerment when you explore and know what brings you pleasure and what your being is capable of experiencing.

The second benefit of masturbation is related to physical health. The Cleveland Clinic (2022) has compiled information from research regarding the impact of masturbation. Benefits include improved sleep, stress reduction, tension relief, increased focus, improved mood, reduction of aches and pain, an enhanced sex life, and a protective factor against anxiety and depression. There is also no risk of getting pregnant from masturbation, and it's only rarely that someone gets a sexually transmitted infection (STI), which often occurs due to sex objects/toys not being properly cleaned after use. When a person orgasms, whether through masturbation or some other means, dopamine and oxytocin are released in the brain, which increase positive emotions in your body. These hormones also counteract the stress hormone cortisol.

Other studies have found that people with penises who ejaculate frequently may have a lower risk of prostate cancer as it helps to prevent the buildup of cancer-causing agents in the prostate gland. Another study found that orgasm resulting from masturbation was shown to boost white blood cells that help fight off infections (Haake et al., 2004). Vulva owners who masturbate are more likely to have an orgasm during partnered sex and can experience some relief from menstrual cramps. In older age, it can help to decrease vaginal dryness, and it helps to decrease pain during intercourse. According to another study, vulva owners who masturbate reported more orgasms, higher self-esteem, increased sexual libido, and overall greater satisfaction with their marriage and sex life (Rowland et al., 2020). Seeing all these benefits makes it difficult for me to see masturbation as something inherently evil since God created us with bodies and brains that are so responsive to pleasure.

I will note, here, that research also found some unwanted side effects from masturbation while noting that the benefits well outnumber the potentially negative side effects. These include guilt or shame due to religious or cultural beliefs, the potential for healthy masturbation to turn into a compulsive behavior (people often use the language "addicted" to describe this), minor physical harm such as chafing, soreness, swelling, or reduced sexual sensitivity if masturbation has been done in an aggressive manner (Zimmer and Imhoff, 2020). Most side effects can be addressed fairly easily and likely will not cause any lasting harm.

While religion often focuses on sex as something absolutely corrupted, it often forgets that there is a spiritual dimension or sacredness to it. This is the third benefit of masturbation. That is, some researchers and scholars suggest that sexual desire is part of a divinely placed longing for a deeper communion with other persons and with God (Grenz, 1997; Smedes,1994). What if we saw sexual desire as a mirror image of God's pursuit of God's own communion with others? What if God's longing to be in communion with creation is a model for our deep longing for intimacy? Certainly, the doctrine of the Trinity is a model of inter-relationship and inter-connection. It's a very tangible expression of a God-in-communion. There are also scripture passages and biblical narratives that promote this theme, and one might conclude that the sexual longing of people, including those who masturbate, does indeed reflect a holy yearning for intimacy that speaks to one's own hope of communion with God. Maybe seeing the benefit of masturbation as a behavior that may actually model the wanting of right relationships with God and others gives us pause to approach this behavior as something that is a needed part of development of a whole being.

In Ecclesiastes chapter three, there is a verse that teaches of being happy, doing good, eating and drinking, and finding satisfaction in all that is undertaken – that this is a gift from God. We see here that humans experiencing pleasure is good. Later in Ecclesiastes (7:17-18), the writer notes, "Don't be overly wicked and don't be a fool...It is good to grasp the one and not let go of the other." This passage is warning a person not to give into extremes and to pursue a safe path. Coupled with one's ability to gain wisdom through prayer and meditation, the teaching in these passages leads me to consider that God gives us the ability to know our boundaries, motivations, and purposes in the act of self-pleasure.

Sexually Explicit Material

Oftentimes, when a person masturbates, they may use a stimulus (this is not true for everyone) known as sexually explicit material (SEM). SEM can include pornography, literature, music, or art. Honestly, many things can be considered SEM if we think of this as anything that causes sexual arousal. It might be easy to jump to the conclusion that SEM is to be rejected in all ways, shape, and form. The church embraced this sentiment since the beginning of SEM. People often see the compulsive use of SEM destroy families, and there is documented research that, depending on the content of SEM, violence towards other humans is the end result. There are indubitably forms of SEM that are evil, create more evil in this world (human trafficking, abuse, exploitation), or are created for the purpose of capitalism and consumerism. Sexually explicit material has harmed people who are in exploitative pornography or view it.

But I want to be curious about the possibility that there is room for gray as it relates to SEM. There might be many arguments against this coming up for you, but I invite you to suspend this judgment for a moment and to give yourself permission to be open. We live in a culture that prioritizes male sexuality over female sexuality, and it teaches that women's pleasure doesn't belong to women and that we should see the ultimate act of sexual pleasure as penetrative sex. Combined with a lack of anatomical self-awareness or having your sex education provided by a male partner (who at times may be providing education regarding how to provide pleasure rather than receive it), the belief that women's pleasure doesn't belong to them leads to women feeling censored and castigated for expressing desire. Women are not taught to have desire, let alone to voice desire. In this way, SEM can help to create vocabulary, imagery, and independence as a woman begins to vicariously explore her own sexuality through the narrative of a character, storyline, or visual aid.

Historically, males have had more access to fantasies and SEM because the pornography world is built for male pleasure. If you've ever found your way to a sexually explicit website, then you've seen categories with headings specifically related to how a female might present in a sexual situation from a male's point of view (i.e., headings that are identified by body parts, stereotypical gender roles, or how much a female "needs" a male). What if SEM could change this pattern? In an NPR interview, author Katherine Rowland noted, "Men can and should play a central role in helping women fully engage with their (women's) desires and sensations. They can do this by being compassionate and nonjudgmental listeners. By creating an erotic atmosphere in which men and women's needs command equal importance and by encouraging interactions that depart from the wearied script of male arousal and release. Just as society tends to overly complicate female sexuality, we oversimplify men's, and they (men) also benefit from shifting dynamics around" (Gharib, 2020).

It is unlikely that either person in this dynamic that follows Christian sexual scripts will know how to suddenly be able to "create an erotic atmosphere." To gain this result, one might benefit from engaging with SEM such as ethical pornography, which is pornography created legally (no underage actors, no trafficking) where there is fair pay, respect, and safe conditions for all performers/sex workers (i.e., STI testing). Consent for all parties is also prioritized. Ethical pornography also pays attention to representation (all bodies and abilities are displayed), and it is not centered around the "male gaze" but takes into account pleasure for all viewers. This type of pornography is typically one that costs money or you need a subscription in order to engage with, which also helps to ensure that the pornography you consume is high quality, ethical, and a secure website. The money you pay goes to the actual sex worker or performer, and paying for this SEM contributes to a safer, more ethical, environment in pornography more broadly. A list of ethical porn sites can be found at the end of this chapter.

To be clear, I am not saying that the only way a person can gain sexual knowledge or support in identifying desire or the fantasies that arouse them is through visual pornography. There are other options such as reading erotic stories (often called erotica), which incorporate many of the same fantasies as visual SEM but do not include real people or visual images. This can often decrease much of the concern that pornography brings up. Erotica presents imaginary narratives that can create space for a person to begin to envision their own fantasies. Scenes presented in reading provide the "permission" many people are not given to explore a personal sexuality or envision themselves trying sexual acts, and these stories can be "both empowering and potentially subversive of both dominant sexist and anti-pornography feminist placements of heterosexual women's relationship to the domain of pornography" (Sonnet, 1999, p. 182). In this vein, erotica offers people a space that can enhance sexuality and sexual well-being. Other ways to enhance sexuality could include exchanging explicit texts/images with a partner to share fantasies or build desire, planning out an upcoming sexual experience to incorporate elements of one another's fantasies, and, of course, more foreplay. Do not forget the importance of extensive foreplay. Not only does this heighten arousal, but it gives each partner time to become aroused and more attentive to the desires had for self and for a partner.

In addition, SEM is shown to have a multitude of effects on people, specifically women. Whether we like it or not, women often become trapped in traditional, Western, gender roles (i.e., mothers, wives, sacrificial, constant caregiver). With this at play, SEM used for the purpose of physical, sexual, or erotic pleasure can be seen as resistance. It is a form of resistance in that it means we disengage physically from the daily tasks of chores, children, and making meals in order to create "space to engage in one's [sexual] imagination" (Smith, 2012 p.159). How can a woman know what she wants if there is never time to disengage from the constant demand to give to all those who would take? How do we become sexual, let alone have sexual agency, if we do not value and take time to independently explore our bodies and sexuality? What is desire if we cannot act on it?

Some research suggests that when women can explore their bodies and sexualities (i.e., their turn-ons, what arousal feels like, how, when, and who they might want to be touched by) they are in a better position to utilize sexual outlets or activities positively in the future (Montemurro, 2014). Not every person may utilize SEM as an aid to learn about the erotic they may hold, but there are several benefits for women who utilize SEM. Recent research suggests that SEM can help women discover aspects of their erotic self, learn about sexualities and sexual practices, gain a sense of sexual empowerment, learn and accept one's body and identities, and gain sexual education and instruction for certain sexual activities or positions (Chesser, Parry, and Light 2019). This same research mentions that erotic empowerment can be a benefit from SEM consumption, arousal, and masturbation.

Empowerment can occur by knowing that you were self-motivated and freely chose what you consumed because it was driven by personal preferences and highlights personal agency. No one can tell you what material you can or cannot read, watch, or engage with. This is something that gets to be just for you. How freeing to purposefully engage in something related to our bodies within a world where women are constantly told what to do or not do with their bodies. You are allowed to be a sexual being. You are allowed to explore your own body. You are allowed to use your own voice to speak what it is that you want. Using SEM can feel empowering and help to improve or expand how you communicate about sex, which helps to deepen experiences of intimacy with others. It can play an indispensable role in strengthening intimate communication with partners, so that you can speak with confidence and comfort about what your desires encompass.

Finally, I want to bring up erotic writing within biblical narratives. I explored this previously, but there are many sexually explicit mentions within scripture – prostitution, rape, dancing for another's pleasure, and a young Jewish girl who becomes queen after just one night with the king (if you know what I mean). Perhaps the most well-known of these narratives is Song of Solomon, which is located within the wisdom literature of the Bible (you can take a moment to think about that). Richard Rohr (2021) notes that this is biblical erotic poetry while also viewing it as a metaphor for "God's passionate delight in us and pursuit of us." In this narrative, the two lovers leave very little to the imagination as they write out their longings for one another while recounting every inch of one another's bodies – what they see and taste and smell with one another. Both lovers openly give voice to their desire to be wanted by the other, to give pleasure and to receive pleasure. Perhaps this erotic art can show us that there is a space for passionate creativity, for giving breath to the deep ache we have for knowing another body, for knowing our own bodies, and for entering into a story of sexual longing that acknowledges the very human craving for deep pleasure.

Kink

Kink is not a new concept in the slightest. It is found in literature and art dating back to ancient texts (Bolin & Whelehan, 2015). Kink often gets a bad reputation, especially for those who do not understand all that it entails. Christians who think in either/or dualisms may find it more comfortable to believe that any part of kink is sinful, but I am hoping to shed some light and create some nuance around kinkiness. Kink practices may include giving or receiving intense sensation, including but not limited to "pain." However, when pain is involved, it is usually a sensation that brings pleasure with it. Kink also includes eroticizing the expression of power or authority differences between people, being aroused by unusual sensual stimuli (typically involving non-genital body parts or inanimate objects), engagement in role play or dramas of erotic scenarios, and activities that can induce shifts in consciousness (Williams and Sprott, 2022).

When people hear the word kink, they often associate it with BDSM.

BDSM (bondage/discipline, dominance/submission, sadism/masochism) is a significant part of the kinky community, but it is one that is often misunderstood, especially when we consider that many people reference *50 Shades of Grey* when they are trying to understand BDSM (opinion: *50 Shades* portrays an abusive egalitarian dynamic whose foundation is trauma reenactment). In reality, recent studies of the kink population (compared to a non-kinky population) find that they seem to exhibit the same or healthier levels of depression, self-esteem, sexual difficulties, obsessive-compulsive tendencies, attachment, post-traumatic stress, family of origin concerns, personality disorders, anxiety, and overall risk for mental health concerns (Connolly, 2006; Cross & Matheson, 2006; Gemberling et al., 2015; Sandnabba et al., 2002; Richters et al., 2008; Wismeijer & Van Assen, 2013). Additionally, those who practice kink tend to be more open to new experiences, more conscientious, and less neurotic in comparison to the general population (Wismeijer & van Assen, 2013). I do want to note that unlike *50 Shades*, research finds that people who engage in BDSM have similar rates of mental health concerns, similar rates of past trauma, and improved well-being compared to those who do not engage in BDSM. It is often surprising for many to discover that kink and BDSM occur quite commonly with 45-60% of the general public reporting that they have fantasies that incorporate dominance and submission (Jozifkova, 2018). Approximately 10-12% of the general population reports having engaged in kink behaviors at some point in their lives (Joyal and Carpenter, 2017).

Those who are a part of the kink community tend to see BDSM as a large part of the kink identity, oftentimes leading to the two terms being used interchangeably or exclusively (Taormino, 2012; Sagarin, Cutler, Cutler, Lawler-Sagarin, & Matuszewich, 2008). When one takes a closer look at the kink community, what will likely be noticed is a flourishing culture that is guided by the values of acceptance, communication, trust, empowerment, and fulfillment. The foundation of BDSM practices, for example, is consent, and kink-oriented individuals maintain strict values and belief systems to protect those involved, including radical honesty, candid communication, expressed consents, safety practices, trust, and full disclosure of risk (Moore et al., 2018). Oftentimes, kinky people will report that their motivation in engaging in kink is to serve both their own and their relationship's sexual needs as well as to fulfill their need for intimacy and closeness while providing the same for their partner(s) (Sagarin et al., 2019).

So, what does BDSM *actually* look like? Well, the beauty of it is that it can be very individualized to meet the needs of those involved in a kinky experience, but generally, there are three phases that happen during a BDSM experience. The first phase has to do with planning the scene and consent. A scene is a longer, formal activity session where the partner(s) come together to plan what actions will take place, what tools or props will be used, and what limits will be agreed upon. When the scene is enacted, it is known as play (Wiseman, 1996). Play is the second phase, where there may be a voluntary power exchange. Power exchange (a primary component of BDSM) is the consensual negotiated exchange of power from one person to another and utilizes labels such as "dominant," "submissive," or "switch" (meaning a person can move between the roles of submissive and dominant). The third phase of a BDSM experience is known as aftercare. Aftercare is the period following the scene/play time where partner(s) receive physical, emotional, and psychological care from one another.

In addition, a debrief of the play typically occurs where communication regarding the successes or obstacles of the scene are discussed. How aftercare is expressed can vary from cuddling, eating something together, rehydrating, or bathing together. One thing I love about aftercare is that it is seen as an integral part of play. It is rarely skipped over and is not considered optional. A recent study identified that the average scene lasts around 55 minutes while the average aftercare phase lasts about 19 minutes, which means that approximately one-third of the time spent together is focused on aftercare (Ambler et al., 2017). This seems vastly refreshing when many people experience a partner rolling off them and going to sleep rather than continuing intimacy through aftercare.

In conversation, I heard someone say that their kinky side began showing up in childhood when they used their dolls to enact BDSM scenes. At the time, they didn't know that this was not considered "normal" and had no idea that there was language to describe how their mind created these stories. There may be a pull to automatically say that this person had been traumatized or violated in some way and that is why childhood play involved this, but actually, kink-oriented desires/fantasies/play typically arise during normal periods of sexual development happening between childhood and into a person's twenties (Bezreh et al., 2012; Waldura et al., 2016). As adults, kinky people don't seem to report distress associated with their sexual expression, but they do note that most distress comes from mistreatment and discrimination by those who don't understand or participate in the kink community (Wright, 2006).

The benefits of kink are numerous. When looking for the benefits that impact those who are in a relationship, research finds that they report increased feelings of contentment, intimacy, and trust after participating in consensual kink (Sagarin et al., 2008). In addition, there is typically a reduction of physiological distress following a successful scene, and partner(s) note the absence of fear, less guilt and worthlessness, increased respect for partner(s), and a lack of aggression towards a partner (Jozifkova, 2013). Individually, the benefits of kink are much more profound than one might think.

There is a sense of empowerment that can form as one participates in BDSM. For instance, to be safely involved in kink one must learn to communicate likes, dislikes, changes, and use their voice (or in a non-verbal manner) to communicate a boundary. Kink can be an opportunity for a person's personal growth, self-actualization, transformation and healing (Sprott, 2020). Let's take, for example, using kink as a practice in healing from a sexually traumatic experience. Trauma can often silence a person and rob them of desire and safety. Research shows that when a woman is involved in kink, they are routinely encouraged to pursue their desires and become empowered in their sexuality (Tripodi, 2017). When a person experiences trauma, it can sometimes live in the body, especially if it goes unprocessed.

Often, trauma reactions include inability to find a sense of control/stability, inability to be present, and being in a constant state of fight/flight. If someone (and again – this is *not* for everyone) is taking on the role of submissive, then they get to decide the outcome of a scene, they negotiate what they want and they have to say "yes" or "no" for play to occur. In a sense, they willingly give up control knowing they are in a safe and controlled environment. Some people will choose to reenact a traumatic occurrence to re-write the narrative from a place of agency, reframing a narrative so that they feel less like a victim. For others, the use of pain play (bondage, impact toys) allows for an outlet for pain. Physical pain involved in some scenes may have the ability to help move emotional pain from the body. While this can be cathartic for some, it would be incredibly dangerous for others wanting to heal from trauma. That is why it is *imperative* that a person engage in trauma-informed therapeutic care to determine what might aid in the healing process before jumping into BDSM practices.

Involvement in BDSM can foster well-being, improve confidence, release sexual shame, build self-esteem, reduce stress, and help one to build trust with another. It can be liberating and joyous, and I wonder how kink and spirituality might coexist. There is certainly nothing in scripture that states healthy, consensual, imaginative sexual play and exploration between partners is an act of immorality. Again, we see the consequences of purity culture, and we also see how scripture can be taught to promote a specific lifestyle. For instance, we know there are biblical texts that speak of sexual immorality or lasciviousness, but we do not always fully understand the contextualized views of human sexuality when these texts were written. It is usually our bias and lack of knowledge that informs our interpretations of sexual immorality, and we may often connect this immorality to kink or other forms of sexual play. However, I hope there is now a clearer picture that kink involves an incredible amount of planning, consent, negotiation, and full awareness of sexual activity, which is *much* different than a non-kinky version of sex that is influenced by purity culture where a wife believes she should "submit" to her husband, even if her consent is not given.

From both psychological and spiritual perspectives, we long for sexuality to be a sacred and revered part of who we are. We desire to see our bodies and expressions of sexuality as something that connects us to the Creator by placing us in postures of openness, joy, and vulnerability; postures that are often a given in kink culture. Perhaps openness in our sexuality can foster an openness in our spirituality.

Consensual Non-Monogamy

If you thought you might feel uncomfortable reading about kink, then go ahead and start clutching your pearls because we are moving into exploring polyamory or consensual non-monogamy (CNM), terms that can be used interchangeably. The term polyamory wasn't created until the 1990s and, in its simplest form, means many (poly) love (amor). Oftentimes, people will draw the conclusion that CNM is about having sex with anyone whenever you want, regardless of relationship status, and while that may be true for some, that definition doesn't capture the entirety of CNM. People who are in those relationships are likely to define polyamory as composed of relationships or feelings for more than one person at a time with a focus on interpersonal feelings, ethics, and consent. People in CNM relationships are also focused on much more beyond the centralization of sex within these relationships (Cardoso, Pascoal, Maiochi, 2021). I also think it may be helpful to know that CNM is not some "fringe" thing. Two national studies (done in Canada and the U.S.) found that approximately 20% of those who participated in the studies endorsed ever having been in a CNM relationship (Fairbrother et al., 2019; Haupert et al., 2017).

I cannot tell you how much stigma abounds towards CNM. Some of the myths include that those in poly relationships are more likely to contract STI's, be "sexually deviant", harmful to others/society, or less committed in a relationship. None of this is supported by research, but these beliefs continue due to a lack of knowledge or stereotyping. People in non-monogamous relationships actually report higher levels of health and happiness than monogamous folks (Fleckenstein and Cox, 2015). Research identifies some themes as to why someone would be motivated to have a poly lifestyle or relationship: (1) getting needs met that a monogamous relationship cannot address; (2) personal growth and autonomy; (3) identity development and polyamory; (4) expression of political values; (5) exploring minority identities like fluidity or bisexuality; (6) the desire to belong to a community; (7) the desire for sexual diversity; and (8) attachment needs (Hnatkovičová and Bianchi, 2022). All these reasons individually seem quite important, but taken together, it creates a picture of the benefits of this type of intimacy.

In some ways, I can imagine someone breathing a sigh of relief once they find the ability to engage in CNM. Too many times in monogamous relationships, the expectations are unbearable, which I often hear repeatedly from my clients. This leads me to ask myself the question, "How in the world did we get to a place where it is seen as better to expect one person (a partner/spouse) to be the sole person who can meet all your needs?" Imagine having access to multiple partners where your needs are shared, and no one is overwhelmed by expectations. What if we had the freedom to define our "truest self" through a sexual ethic that allows us to see that we might be created to engage with more than one person for the rest of our emotional and sexual lives? In many ways, I can see how a CNM relationship would demand more honesty, acceptance, and humility than a person may typically have in a relationship, thereby pushing us to grow in who we are and how we love. Yet, there are also many drawbacks, as many CNM folk engage in long struggles to address jealousy and to unlearn heteronormative scripts in order to be fully present. But I also think that having a community instead of a partner is something we may be wired for because it addresses our deep need for belonging and inter-connection.

Could there really be a benefit to having emotional and sexual intimacy with multiple partners? Yes and no. Research suggests it is not without challenges due to jealousy and figuring out how to manage multiple emotional bonds simultaneously, but overall, I find myself noticing that the benefits might outweigh the challenges. For instance, we meet people and fall in love with them in the hopes that our psychological needs (like eroticism and nurturance) will be met. Imagine having the ability to have these psychological needs met within multiple relationships (Balzarini et al., 2019). I think it protects against relational burn out, and those who are poly have noted that they experience higher levels of having needs met because different partners can meet different needs.

Another benefit is communication. To be in a poly relationship, there is constant communication and negotiation regarding roles, blending families, addressing jealousy, and learning how to develop "compersion" (being happy because you know your partner is happy and is the opposite of jealousy). Poly folk can show us how to let go of sexual rigidity and embrace flexibility because the existence of CNM relies on people being willing to try new things, adapt to meet their own and others' needs, and discover new patterns of existing and relating (something that monogamous folk may struggle with). Overall, then, the benefits of CNM include connections to sexual novelty, gaining new insight about one's sexual strengths, and desire congruence has a higher likelihood of being aligned, and all of this can occur when you have a deep sexual connection with more than one partner.

Finally, I want to address some biblical narratives that might point us towards a more fluid way of interpreting sexual relationships. When asking most Christians, we may likely hear a response about a rigid monogamy related to Adam and Eve being the first created humans, or someone starting off with "the Bible says____." The Bible truly does say many things, but I don't think it was created to be a rulebook, especially within purity culture, because the Bible seems to be more than simply a listing of purity codes. If we can adjust the lens through which we see the Bible, then we might begin to notice that it is full of stories about relationships. How people relate to themselves, to creation, to pain, and to the Divine. It is not merely a book that tells us what we can do or not do. However, even if we hold this lens and we go looking for words like non-monogamy or polyamory we, of course, will not find them. But we may find some words to consider about relationships. For instance, in the book of Philippians we read, "This is my prayer: that your love might become even more and more rich in knowledge and all kinds of insight." In other passages, we see directives to seek justice, love mercy, and to draw close to God.

In addition, there are scriptures in the Old Testament that do address non-monogamy specifically dictating how it should be done (i.e., caring for wives, dividing inheritances, etc.) rather than stating it is something that should not be done. But, I find myself curious. Could polyamory be tolerated rather than celebrated? I draw a parallel to divorce, for example. The New Testament discusses that this is not ideal, but it is sometimes the path that is chosen, and God tolerates it. By this, I mean that God does not judge a person for divorce or condemn them in some way. What if the same thing is true about polyamory? Or, what if we were to consider that Jesus is polyamorous? In the New Testament, Christians were given an image about God's relationship with us humans. In Ephesians chapter five, there are structures given about heterosexual marriage during that time in history. The section finishes by saying that all those instructions show how Christ loves and cares for the Church. Jesus is married to the entire body of believers. That's the biggest sized polyamorous relationship I've ever heard of, and one with a polyamorous and pansexual Jesus to boot. Keeping in this vein, we might look at the love between Christ and the church and know that all are loved equally, that love for me is not diminished by the love that God has for you. Maybe Jesus gave us something to consider when he showed us how to love multiple people at one time.

Gender Identity

The term "gender identity" didn't exist until after 1960, but we've been talking about it for much longer. Freud's "penis envy" is something he never stopped talking about, but he isn't alone in that because we all seem to be a bit obsessed with it. Who has one? Who doesn't have one? Did you have one when you were born? If a child is born and a doctor looks down for that tiny little phallus, there is a shout, "It's a boy!" (even when this isn't always accurate). Dr. Anne Fausto-Sterling (2018) notes that by birth, a baby actually has five layers of sex based on growth during gestation. She also notes that these layers don't always align with one another, or it doesn't become strictly binary. In fact, the layers can conflict with one another. Such as an XX (in most cases female) baby being born with a penis or an XY (in most cases male) person being born with a vagina. This could lead us to infer that there are complexities in assigning sex as male or female at birth. It may simply not be as simple as looking for the presence or absence of a penis.

Sometimes the concept of gender identity can feel confusing, and it is often mixed up with sexual identity, orientation, or sex. Gender identity is simply what someone feels is their gender, and this identity is not connected to a person's genitals or their outward appearance. Fun fact: if you were to Google gender identities, you would find over 100 identities. Gender is a social construct, not an inherent reality of biology. Gender is not something that can be assumed as it is an internal identity that may or may not correlate with how a person dresses, grooms, or speaks. It may be helpful to know that how a person externally shows up in terms of apparel, hair style, voice, or behaviors is known simply as gender expression (Bloom et al., 2021).

As a psychologist, I've had the privilege to learn about the history of gender and the mental health field. In the 1950s, the first sex-reassignment surgery was completed. At about the same time, Harry Benjamin (a sexologist) reported a case of a "woman kept in the body of a man," which was coined transsexualism. Since then, the field adapted these terms, changing transsexualism to gender identity disorder, which it changed again from gender identity disorder to the most recent term, gender dysphoria. This is defined as a "marked incongruence between their experienced or expressed gender and the one they were assigned at birth" (American Psychiatric Association, 2013). This incongruence, if not addressed, can lead to interpersonal conflicts with family and friends and can also lead to rejection from society, symptoms of depression and anxiety, substance use disorders, a negative sense of well-being, poor self-esteem, and increased risk for suicide and self-harm (Garg, Elshimy, and Marwaha, 2023).

The mental health field changed its language around gender identity and slowly de-pathologized it over time, modeling that this is an aspect of life that can be accepted and no longer demonized. However, it seems gender identity concerns are now going through a renaissance of rejection, where the human rights of people are being taken away from those trying to live in a way that honors the connection they have with themselves. A connection that those outside of this experience struggle to fully grasp. Current day persecution of gender non-conforming or trans people, which is what is happening in 2024 at the time this book is being written, is occurring every day.

In 37 states, lawmakers introduced at least 142 bills to restrict gender-affirming healthcare, and this could look like anything from using preferred names and pronouns to hormone therapy to surgery. These bills are increasing in frequency with nearly three times the number introduced as those in 2022. Eighty percent of those bills target gender-affirming care for trans children under the age of 18, while the rest target people of all ages (Funakoshi and Raychaudhuri, 2023). Penalties outlined in some of these bills include health care professionals losing their ability to practice, parents losing custodial rights of their children, prison sentences of three years to life, and loss of healthcare coverage.

Sadly, when a person is unable to find gender affirming care their inability to access gender-affirming care is shown to increase the odds of a suicide attempt by 73% in transgender folk (Zwickl et al., 2021). In contrast, another study finds that when states have equality reflected in marital laws, lower rates of suicide attempts in transgender and sexual minority youth were found (Coulter et al., 2019). And, while there are many who believe that not enough evidence is available for immediate outcomes of gender-affirming care, we do have some preliminary evidence (from studies conducted between 2015-2020) that receiving gender-affirming care through puberty blockers and hormone therapy was associated with improved psychological functioning, body satisfaction, decreased depression, and decreased suicidality within a 1-year period (Costa et al., 2015; Kuper et al., 2020; Achille et al., 2020; Allen et al., 2019). We also know that it is the small things that can make a significant difference, such as using a person's preferred pronoun, using gender-neutral language, validating others, and showing acceptance, which leads to increased quality of life and hope (Bhatt, Cannella, and Gentile, 2022).

I think people experience resistance, specifically Christians, due to misinformation or disinformation and also because of a white-knuckled hold on scripture stating we are "fearfully and wonderfully made" (Psalm 139:14). We get really caught up with "God doesn't make mistakes," and we use that to point at scripture and say it is wrong to change what God has made you to be. If that is the absolute truth, then what do we make of someone being born with brunette hair coloring it to be blonde? Or, what about someone who gets a face lift, a tummy tuck, or a breast augmentation? Either due to personal desires or maybe in response to illness? Or, what about a person who is so desperate to change their body shape that they live on protein and pre-workout? These examples may seem innocuous, but do they not also symbolize changes that constitute rejection of being "fearfully and wonderfully made?" Is it just that these changes are commonplace and acceptable? Why do we demonize someone who grows within their own body, who knows their own soul, and decides one day, "What I was born with isn't congruent with who I am truly meant to be." We are okay with growth and transformation – even being "born again" into new life so that our old self passes away – as long as it's the "right" transformation.

I am curious about how the image of God fits into gender. When I think of the image of God, I believe that this image reflects the diversity found in all Creation. In Genesis, we see that God declared all Creation good and that all of Creation is made in God's image, not just humans. If God's image is in everything, then can we not wonder how it shows up in trans folks or non-binary people? Linguistically in scripture, "God" is male, but God's "Spirit" is a bit more fluid. In Hebrew, *ruah* is feminine and means both "spirit" and "breath." In Aramaic, "spirit" is also feminine. In Greek, *pneuma* is neuter and means both "spirit" and "breath" – the same Spirit that moves over the waters of the deep in Genesis, the same Spirit that descends on Jesus at his baptism, the same Spirit that comes down during Pentecost as flaming tongues of fire. God's image appears in all of us meaning that those with diverse genders are as much a part of the image of God as anyone else. If we look, we see many examples in scripture of inclusion and acceptance of diversity.

In the New Testament, the Church is called the bride of Christ, effectively making everyone within the church female and thus gender fluid. Paul also tells us to let go of our dualistic thinking, such as male and female, which could indicate a non-binary approach to Christian subjectivity and identity formation since it is no longer "I" who live but (a type of mystically androgynous) Christ who lives in me. Supported by this is Paul's teaching on putting on the mind of Christ so that we learn to see differently, beyond our dualisms that only lead to judgment and blame, and he also teaches us that all are equally accepted into the mystical Body of Christ through grace. Some are hands, and some are feet. We all have our role to play, but there are no exclusions. We also see examples of gender non-conforming folk in scripture.

In the Old Testament, we see Deborah who is a warrior, the only female judge in her time, performing roles that were historically held by men. Some scholars also suggest that some texts point to Joseph being gender-queer, that the coat of many colors was a female garment (Harris, 2019). We even have a brief mention of a man carrying a jar of water in the Passion narrative, a task typically delegated to women. Lastly, we see how God (in a kind of weird story) showed us a powerful story of inclusivity with the Ethiopian Eunuch in Acts. Here, we have a eunuch (sexual minority) seeking to understand God. By the end of this story, we hear the eunuch ask if anything is standing in the way of baptism, and we are shown that there was no reason this eunuch could not receive full membership into the church. There is no discussion about the gender identity, sexual orientation, or race of this person. Philip (who met with the eunuch) doesn't have any "hate the sin, not the sinner" talk and instead says, "If you believe with your heart you are welcome here."

God doesn't make mistakes – this is something I have heard hundreds of times. Do we take this to mean that since you were born with a certain type of genitalia this represents God not making mistakes? Or, perhaps a person who has the courage and insight to know that their gender is not congruent with their internal experience and chooses to find a way to live more congruently is an image-bearer of God. Perhaps they are the ones who finally express their sacred humanity by bearing witness to the aliveness within them is an example of God not making mistakes.

Sexual Orientation

Results from a 2022 Pew Research Center indicate that 7.2% of U.S. adults identify as LGBTQ+ (Brown, 2023). This translates to approximately 20 million adults. Many of these adults have stories about how a faith identity greatly impacted their understanding of a personal sexuality in a manner that was destructive and, at times, traumatic. However, religious interpretation of human sexuality is not the only issue. The field of psychology offered its own challenges for those within the LGBTQ+ community. Homosexuality, for example, was classified under "sociopathic personality disturbance" in the first edition of the DSM (the manual used to diagnose psychiatric disorders). In the third edition of the DSM, it was considered a psychiatric disorder until 1973 when it was no longer included in the DSM-3, but it has been a part of the DSM until the fifth edition, which is the most recent. Regardless that the psychological community no longer sees queerness as a disorder, the effects of how LGBTQ+ people were "cured" by pseudo-science continues to this day.

Historically, "homosexuality," which I will call queerness, goes back to 2400 B.C.E. in what is to be believed as the first same-sex couple in recorded history between Khnumhotep and Niankhkhnum (Schott, 2016). In the history of the Protestant U.S. the persecution of LGBTQ folk began in 1624 when Richard Cornish of the Virginia Colony was tried and hanged for sodomy; however, in his case, sexual assault was involved, which makes it difficult to know if the punishment he received was for assault or the act of sodomy. The presence of LGBTQ folks is woven into the fabric of this country's history, but unfortunately, early information about its role was not recorded as identification of LGBTQ folk, which can lead to negative consequences. Oftentimes, what is recorded is the ostracizing or persecution that was endured for being what was often considered "sinful." The constant exclusion of queerness is often promoted by religious organizations and, ultimately, led to the gay rights movement that is still present as we continue to see new laws meant to stifle the rights of LGBTQ individuals. For decades, the conservative church made the opposition of same-sex marriage a chief issue for religion in the U.S., often led by Christian activists, such as Jerry Falwell, Anita Bryant, and James Dobson, whose shouted messages characterized queerness as a threat to the "traditional family."

Enter Joseph Nicolosi Sr., the father of reparative therapy, which is one of the most damaging therapies that emerged from the field of psychology. Nicolosi practiced this pseudo-scientific therapy he reported came from the field of psychoanalysis. He claimed that reparative therapy (also known as conversion therapy) could help individuals mitigate or eliminate homosexual desires and replace them with heterosexual ones. His theory was that homosexuality was a condition that came from a perceived rejection or detachment from a same-sex meaningful person such as a parent. He thought that this detachment led to an interruption of a typical masculine or feminine identification development (Nicolosi, 2004). His thought was that this interruption was the "trauma" that would cause a person to become queer through the "erotic reenactment of the love-hate relationship" and felt it was his calling to restore "that which functions in accordance with its biological design" (Nicolosi, 2016). I have watched many videos of Nicolosi's sessions with clients he is "curing," and sadly, they often entail a significant amount of emotional manipulation and the weaponizing of someone's emotional trauma to inflict more distress until a "release" of emotions occurs.

From Nicolosi's work, the field of conversion therapy began, although practices trying to convert sexuality were used for centuries. Conversion therapy was sold as a form of therapy that could convert a gay person to heterosexuality. These pseudo-therapies had no scientific backing and were often set up as ministries rather than therapeutic treatments. Conversion therapy took many forms, from discussions, talks, and conferences that focused on toxic masculinity and discouragement of queer identity (Community-Based Research Center, 2020), but there were numerous egregious forms of conversion therapy that included shock therapy, exorcisms, and primal therapy (Ford, 2002; Ludwig, 2016; Streed Jr, Anderson, Babits, & Ferguson, 2019).

Other techniques used in conversion therapy included praying, reading "educational materials," attending Bible studies, and attending group therapies aimed as suppressing queer identity and expression (Flentje & Chohran, 2013). The point of all these treatments was to convince those involved that heterosexual and cisgendered identities are preferable, if not more accepted by God, than LGBTQ identities. Imagine believing that you are inherently bad. You were created wrong and who you are needs to be completely erased for you to be accepted by others and by God. It is staggering when we think of the 698,000 adults in the U.S. that experienced conversion therapy either from a therapist or a religious advisor, with about 350,000 of those people going through conversion therapy as an adolescent (The Williams Institute, 2018).

Many of the larger-known conversion therapy ministries such as Exodus and JONAH are disbanded, but we continue to see religious institutions take the lead in promoting the conversion of sexuality. These ministries can range from individual pastoral counseling to "ex-gay" group gatherings and retreat programs (Brush, 2021), and while almost every professional licensing board in the U.S. denounces conversion therapy, religious organizations are exempt from the oversight of their practice as they are not beholden to licensing boards or ethical standards of care. Religious organizations use religion and the second amendment to hide themselves from oversight and accountability (Brush, 2021). However, it is reported that some of these practices include holding people (often the vulnerable, like minors) against their will. Some might call this kidnapping.

I would like to think that the age of conversion therapy is over, and that Christians and non-Christians will find a way to accept that we are each created uniquely and that there is nothing we could do to have God love us less. Unfortunately, the unjust practice of conversion therapy is still breathing. Based on research from The Williams Institute (2018), we can expect that 16,000 LGBTQ adolescents (ages 13-17) will be subject to conversion therapy from a licensed health care professional before they reach the age of 18 in the 32 states that still have not banned the practice of conversion therapy. Approximately 10,000 LGBTQ adolescents (ages 13 – 17) who live in one of the states with conversion therapy bans are protected from enduring therapy from a licensed healthcare professional before the age of 18, and an estimated 57,000 adolescents across all states will be treated with conversion therapy by a religious or spiritual advisor before the age of 18. This is devastating as the copious amounts of research identifying the impact of conversion therapy finds that adolescents who undergo therapy are twice as likely to report attempting suicide or having multiple suicide attempts (Green et al., 2020). Furthermore, the immediate effects of conversion therapy include feelings of inauthenticity, forced and pretend acceptance of biological sex, forced or pretend conformed gender norms, and long-term effects include a loss of faith, lack of trust in others, sexual dysfunction, and poor self-esteem (Tillewein & Kruse-Diehr, 2023).

The trauma that is experienced in the name of the ex-gay movement is astronomical. Terms such as "pray the gay away" simply do not lead to all people becoming heterosexual, and why would we do this when we know a person's sexuality is designed and given by a loving God. Psalm 139:13-14, for example, tells us that all components of a person's identity and being are as carefully knit together by God. Or, in the New Testament, we see that God welcomes people of all genders and sexual identities when it teaches us, "There is neither Jew nor Gentile, neither slave nor free, nor is there male and female (neither gay nor straight, transgender nor cisgender), for you are all one in Christ Jesus" (Galatians 3:28).

Richard Rohr (2019) discusses how God is more comfortable with diversity than humans are, and this is evidenced by the cosmos being about two things: people and things becoming themselves (differentiation) and living in supportive coexistence (communion). He goes on to state that those who are homophobic or anti-gay might seem to have well-supported arguments, but these arguments are secular. Their arguments may be called "biblically based," but they are not. They are secular because they focus on control, majority rule, fear of others and the unknown, and the idealization of a "traditional family." Jesus did not have a "traditional family," nor did he promote a traditional family in any of his teachings.

What Jesus showed us was the simplistic teachings that we are to love God and to love other people (Matthew 22:35-40). This simple yet powerful directive can be expanded to show that there is freedom for people to love God and to love others in a way that is individual, creative, maybe outside the norm, and driven by the shape of one's soul. I don't think God really cares about who makes up a relationship as the focus is all about union. The kind we form with God and with others. We are not to become hindered by labels – woman, man, trans, cis, bisexual, straight, queer – but to see that we all belong. That there is perfect union available through God. Jesus is constantly and consistently affirming, much like the cosmos itself, and these two parallel drives towards diversity and communion are what is ordained by God (Rohr, 2019).

Closing

My hope is that this chapter made you uncomfortable. My assumption is that many of us ran as fast as we could to the dualistic parts of our minds where we found our either/or answers and wanted very much to stay in this safety. There is nothing wrong with that. In some ways, our minds were created to find answers and reason as fast as possible to decrease chaos and uncertainty. But I also hope you were able to consider what it would be like to live in the gray – the space where we learn that we don't have to know the answers, that there isn't always a "right or wrong" but more of a wondering about what fits with the spirit and soul God created within us. With an open spirit, we have the freedom to see how sexuality can attune us more to the longings we were endowed with, and that these longings can move us into a deeper communion with the Divine.

Get Curious

1. After reading this chapter, re-write what thoughts or values you hold about the following subjects:

    - Masturbation
    - Sexually explicit materials
    - Kink
    - Consensual non-monogamy
    - Gender identity
    - Sexual orientation

2. Notice if any of your opinions changed from before you read this chapter.

3. Are there things that stirred a longing in you while reading this chapter? Is there a way for you to keep leaning into that longing with openness and non-judgment?

Ethical Pornography Materials

Bellesa.co: A pornography company run by women and whose films cater to women. They offer videos, cams, and written erotic stories. "At Bellesa we believe that sexuality on the internet should depict women as we truly are—as subjects of pleasure, not objects of conquest," according to their website.

XConfessions and Lust Cinema: A female-owned company whose website states, "Every explicit movie you'll find here is visually arresting, goes beyond traditional gender roles and tired stereotypes. We push the boundaries of fetish, lust, desire and intimacy. Plus, every movie is accompanied by behind-the-scenes footage, on-set performer & director interviews, and exclusive photos. We're really proud of how we make our movies, and we want you to be able to see exactly how they were made."

BrightDesire: All of the things we love about sex: the intimacy, the fun, the passion. The platform includes scenes of real-life couples exploring themselves sexually and embracing the pleasure they feel without a script. The films are described as holistic and are more than just a focus on genitals and tries to capture the smaller intimate moments of sex.

Joybear: A British film production company. The website states, "We have been making sex-positive, erotic films since 2003. Our goal is to change the perception of the adult entertainment business."

Make Love Not Porn: This site shows what real sex looks like, in every flavor. Real couples and individuals can send in their erotic videos and get paid for them. People/Users/Contributors can remain anonymous if they choose, and they can also remove their videos from the platform at any time.

Dipsea: Audio porn that celebrates healthy sex by offering clips for every flavor, interest, or fantasy. Scripts are written in-house, and the company partners with voice actors—all of which are paid. Yearly subscriptions start at $70.

Frolicme: Created with couples and people with vulvas in mind. This platform depicts the art of mutually consenting sex between adults with a focus on female pleasure and passion. This site offers adult films, erotic articles, and erotic audio.

Sssh: A crowdsourced erotic film platform that dives into the fantasies and desires shared among their members by combining porn and artistry. This site brings stories that stimulate both the mind and body by using techniques like virtual reality (VR) and narrative.

Chapter Four References

Achille, C., Taggart, T., Eaton, N. R., Osipoff, J., Tafuri, K., Lane, A., & Wilson, T. A. (2020). Longitudinal impact of gender-affirming endocrine intervention on the mental health and well-being of transgender youths: preliminary results. *International Journal of Pediatric Endocrinology*, 1, 1-5.

Allen, L. R., Watson, L. B., Egan, A. M., & Moser, C. N. (2019). Well-being and suicidality among transgender youth after gender-affirming hormones. *Clinical Practice in Pediatric Psychology*, 7(3), 302.

Ambler, J. K., Lee, E. M., Klement, K. R., Loewald, T., Comber, E. M., Hanson, S. A., & Sagarin, B. J. (2017). Consensual BDSM facilitates role-specific altered states of consciousness: a preliminary study. *Psychology of Consciousness: Theory, Research, and Practice*, 4(1), 75–91. doi: 10.1037/cns0000097.

American Psychiatric Association (2013). *Diagnostic and statistical manual of mental disorders* (5th ed.). doi: 10.1176/appi.books.9780890425596.

Balzarini, R. N., Dharma, C., Muise, A., & Kohut, T. (2019). Eroticism versus nurturance: how eroticism and nurturance differs in polyamorous and monogamous relationships. *Social Psychology*, 50(3), 185–200. doi: 10.1027/1864-9335/a000378.

Bezreh, T., Weinberg, T. S., & Edgar, T. (2012). BDSM disclosure and stigma management: Identifying opportunities for sex education. *American Journal of Sexuality Education*, 7(1), 37–61. doi: 10.1080/15546128.2012.650984.

Bhatt, N., Cannella, J., & Gentile, J. P. (2022). Gender-affirming care for transgender patients. *Innovations in Clinical Neuroscience*, 19(4-6), 23–32.

Bloom, T. M., Nguyen, T. P., Lami, F., Pace, C. C., Poulakis, Z., Telfer, M., & Tollit, M. A. (2021). Measurement tools for gender identity, gender expression, and gender dysphoria in transgender and gender-diverse children and adolescents: a systematic review. *The Lancet Child & Adolescent Health*, 5(8), 582-588.

Bolin, A. & Whelehan, P. (Eds.) (2015). *The international encyclopedia of human sexuality*. John Wiley & Sons, Ltd. doi: **10.1002/9781118896877. wbiehs043**.

Brown, A. (2023, June 23). 5 key findings about LGBTQ+ Americans. *Pew Research Center*. Retrieved from https://www.pewresearch.org/short-reads/2023/06/23/5-key-findings-about-lgbtq-americans.

Brush, J. (2021, January 29). Conversion ministries and ex-gay ministries. *Ohio Psychological Association*. Retrieved from https://ohpsych.org/news/549803/Conversion-Ministries-and-Ex-Gay-Ministries.htm.

Cardoso, D., Pascoal, P. M., & Maiochi, F. H. (2021). Defining polyamory: a thematic analysis of lay people's definitions. *Archives of Sexual Behavior*, 50(4), 1239–1252. doi: **10.1007/s10508-021-02002-y**.

Catholic Church (2000). *Catechism of the catholic church* (2nd ed.). Our Sunday Visitor.

Chesser, S., Parry, D., & Penny Light, T. (2019). Nurturing the erotic self: benefits of women consuming sexually explicit materials. *Sexualities*, 22(7–8), 1234–1252. doi: **10.1177/1363460718791898**.

The LATEST: Conversion Therapy & SOGIECE in Canada (2020). *Community-Based Research Center*. Retrieved from https://www.cbrc.net/sex_now_survey_results_reveal_prevalence_of_change_efforts.

Connolly, P. H. (2006). Psychological functioning of bondage/domination/sado-masochism (BDSM) practitioners. *Journal of Psychology & Human Sexuality*, 18(1), 79–120. doi: **10.1300/j056v18n01_05**.

Conversion Therapy and LGBT Youth (2018). *The Williams Institute, UCLA School of Law*. The Williams Institute.

Costa, R., Dunsford, M., Skagerberg, E., Holt, V., Carmichael, P., & Colizzi, M. (2015). Psychological support, puberty suppression, and psychosocial functioning in adolescents with gender dysphoria. *The Journal of Sexual Medicine*, 12(11), 2206-2214.

Coulter, R. W., Egan, J. E., Kinsky, S., Friedman, M. R., Eckstrand, K. L., Frankeberger, J., & Miller, E. (2019). Mental health, drug, and violence interventions for sexual/gender minorities: a systematic review. *Pediatrics*, 144(3).

Cross, P., & Matheson, K. (2006). Understanding sadomasochism: an empirical examination of four perspectives. *Journal of Homosexuality*, 50, 133-166.

Fairbrother, N., Hart, T. A., & Fairbrother, M. (2019). Open relationship prevalence, characteristics, and correlates in a nationally representative sample of Canadian adults. *Journal of Sex Research*, 56(6), 695–704. doi: 10.1080/00224499.2019.1580667.

Fausto-Sterling, A. (2018, October 25). Why sex is not binary. *The New York Times*, Section A, 19. Retrieved from https://www.nytimes.com/2018/10/25/opinion/sex-biology-binary.html.

Fleckenstein, J. R. & Cox, D. W. (2015). The association of an open relationship orientation with health and happiness in a sample of older US adults. *Sexual and Relationship Therapy*, 30(1):94–116. doi: 10.1080/14681994.2014.976997.

Flentje, A., Heck, N. C., & Cochran, B. N. (2013). Sexual reorientation therapy interventions: perspectives of ex-ex-gay individuals. *Journal of Gay & Lesbian Mental Health*, 17(3), 256-277.

Ford, J. G. (2002). Healing homosexuals: a psychologist's journey through the ex-gay movement and the pseudo-science of reparative therapy. *Journal of Gay & Lesbian Psychotherapy*, 5(3-4), 69-86.

Funakoshi, M. & Raychaudhuri, D. (2023, August 19). The rise of anti-trans bills in the US. *Reuters*. Retrieved September 29, 2023, from https://www.reuters.com/graphics/USA-HEALTHCARE/TRANS-BILLS/zgvorreyapd/.

Garg, G., Elshimy, G., & Marwaha, R. (2023) *Gender dysphoria*. [Updated 2023, Jul 11]. StatPearls Publishing.

Gemberling, T. M., Cramer, R. J., Wright, S., & Nobels, M. R. (2015). Psychological functioning and violence victimization and perpetration in BDSM practitioners from the national coalition for sexual freedom (Tech. Rep.). *National Coalition for Sexual Freedom*. Retrieved from https://pdfs.semanticscholar.org/0cd8/ abb591fda8685091c1f208bc757d616f0903.pdf.

Gharib, M. (Host). (2020, February 14). Real orgasms and transcendent pleasure: How women are reigniting desire. *NPR* [Radio broadcast episode]. Retrieved from https://www.npr.org/sections/health-shots/2020/02/14/803725591/real-orgasms-and-transcendent-pleasure-how-women-are-reigniting-desire.

Grenz, S. J. (1997). *Sexual ethics: An Evangelical perspective*. Westminster John Knox Press.

Green, A. E., Price-Feeney, M., Dorison, S. H., & Pick, C. J. (2020). Self-reported conversion efforts and suicidality among US LGBTQ youths and young adults, 2018. *American Journal of Public Health*, 110(8), 1221–1227. doi: 10.2105/AJPH.2020.305701.

Haake, P., Krueger, T. H., Goebel, M. U., Heberling, K. M., Hartmann, U., & Schedlowski, M. (2004). Effects of sexual arousal on lymphocyte subset circulation and cytokine production in man. *Neuroimmunomodulation*, 11(5), 293–298. doi: 10.1159/000079409.

Harris, R. (2019). Sexual orientation in the presentation of Joseph's character in biblical and rabbinic literature. *AJS Review*, 43(1), 67-104. doi: 10.1017/S0364009419000035.

Haupert, M. L., Gesselman, A. N., Moors, A. C., Fisher, H. E., & Garcia, J. R. (2017). Prevalence of experiences with consensual nonmonogamous relationships: findings from two national samples of single Americans. *Journal of Sex and Marital Therapy*, 43(5), 424–440. doi: 10.1080/0092623X.2016.1178675.

Hnatkovičová, D. & Bianchi, G. (2022) Model of motivations for engaging in polyamorous relationships. *Sexologies*, 31(3), 184-194. doi: 10.1016/j.sexol.2022.03.003.

Joyal, C. C. & Carpentier, J. (2017). The prevalence of paraphilic interests and behaviors in the general population: a provincial survey. *The Journal of Sex Research*, 54(2), 161–171. doi: 10.1080/00224499.2016.1139034.

Jozifkova, E. (2018). Sexual arousal by dominance and submissiveness in the general population: how many, how strongly, and why. *Deviant Behavior* 39(9), 1229–1236. doi: 10.1080/01639625.2017.1410607.

Kinsey, A. C., Pomeroy, W. B., & Martin, C. E. (1948). *Sexual behavior in the human male*. W. B. Saunders.

Kinsey, A. C., Pomeroy, W. B., & Martin, C. E. (1953). *Sexual behavior in the human female*. W. B. Saunders.

Kuper, L. E., Stewart, S., Preston, S., Lau, M., & Lopez, X. (2020). Body dissatisfaction and mental health outcomes of youth on gender-affirming hormone therapy. *Pediatrics*, 145(4).

Kwee, A. W. & Hoover, D. C. (2008). Theologically-informed education about masturbation: a male sexual health perspective. *Journal of Psychology and Theology*, 36(4), 258–269. doi: 10.1177/009164710803600402.

Landon, S. (2016). "In the beginning: Sexual history." In *Gay awareness: discovering the heart of the father and the mind of Christ on sexuality*. Famous Publishing.

Ludwig, C. (2016). Conversion therapy, its detrimental consequences, and its place in the national spotlight. *Rutgers JL & Religion*, 18, 121.

Montemurro, B. (2014) *Deserving desire: Women's stories of sexual evolution*. Rutgers University Press.

Moore, L., Pincus, T., & Rodemaker, D. (2018). What professionals need to know about BDSM. *National Coalition for Sexual Freedom*. Retrieved from https://www.ncsfreedom.org/images/stories/pdfs/Activist/What_Professionals_Need_to_Know_About_BDSM_1.pdf.

Numbers, Ronald L. (2003). "Sex, science, and salvation: The sexual advice of Ellen G. White and John Harvey Kellogg." In *Right Living: An Anglo-American tradition of self-help medicine and hygiene*. Charles Rosenberg (Ed.), pp. 208-209.

Nicolosi, J. (2004). *Reparative therapy of male homosexuality*. Rowman & Littlefield.

Nicolosi, J. (2016). The traumatic foundation of male homosexuality. *Crisis Magazine*. Retrieved from https://crisismagazine.com/opinion/traumatic-foundation-male-homosexuality.

Richters, J., Visser, R. O. D., Rissel, C. E., Grulich, A. E., & Smith, A. M. (2008). Demographic and psychosocial features of participants in bondage and discipline, "sadomasochism" or dominance and submission (BDSM): Data from a national survey. *The Journal of Sexual Medicine*, 5(7), 1660–1668. doi: 10.1111/j.1743-6109.2008.00795.x.

Rohr, R. (2021, June 8). Biblical erotic poetry. *Center for Action and Contemplation*. Retrieved September 17, 2023, from https://cac.org/daily-meditations/biblical-erotic-poetry-2021-06-08/.

Rohr, R. (2019, October 15). Diversity and communion. *Center for Action and Contemplation*. Retrieved October 24, 2023, from https://cac.org/daily-meditations/diversity-and-communion-2019-10-21/.

Rowland, D. L., Kolba, T. N., McNabney, S. M., Uribe, D., & Hevesi, K. (2020). Why and how women masturbate, and the relationship to orgasmic response, *Journal of Sex & Marital Therapy*, 46(4), 361-376. doi: 10.1080/0092623X.2020.1717700.

Sagarin, B. J., Cutler, B., Cutler, N., Lawler-Sagarin, K. A., & Matuszewich, L. (2008). Hormonal changes and couple bonding in consensual sadomasochistic activity. *Archives of Sexual Behavior*, 38(2), 186–200. doi: 10.1007/s10508-008-9374-5.

Sagarin, B. J., Lee, E. M., Erickson, J. M. et al. (2019). Collective sex environments without the sex? Insights from the BDSM community. *Archives of Sexual Behavior*, 48, 63–67. doi: **10.1007/s10508-018-1252-1.**

Sandnabba, N. K., Santtila, P., Alison, L., & Nordling, N. (2002). Demographics, sexual behaviour, family background and abuse experiences of practitioners of sadomasochistic sex: a review of recent research. *Sexual and Relationship Therapy*, 17(1), 39– 55. doi: 10.1080/14681990220108018.

Shryock, R. H. (1931). Sylvester Graham and the Popular Health Movement, 1830-1870. *The Mississippi Valley Historical Review*, 18(2), 172–183. doi: **10.2307/1893378.**

Smedes, L. B. (1994). *Sex for Christians* (Rev. Ed.).: W. B. Eerdmans.

Smith, C. (2012). "I guess they got past their fear of porn: women viewing porn films" In Mendik X (Ed.), *Peep Shows: Cult Film and the Cine-Erotic*. Wallflower Press, pp. 155–167.

Sonnet, E. (1999). Erotic fiction by women for women: the pleasures of post-feminist heterosexuality, *Sexualities*, 2(2), 167–187.

Sprott, R. A. (2020). Reimagining "kink": Transformation, growth, and healing through BDSM. *Journal of Humanistic Psychology*. doi: 10.1177/0022167819900036.

Streed, Jr., C. G., Anderson, J. S., Babits, C., & Ferguson, M. A. (2019). Changing medical practice, not patients-putting an end to conversion therapy. *The New England Journal of Medicine*, 381(6), 500-502.

Taormino, T. (2012). *The ultimate guide to kink: bdsm, role play and the erotic edge.* Cleis Press.

Tillewein, H. & Kruse-Diehr, A. J. (2023). The impact of sexual orientation conversion therapies on transgender individuals. *Psychology & Sexuality*, 1-13.

Waldura, J. F., Arora, I., Randall, A. M., Farala, J. P., & Sprott, R. A. (2016). Fifty shades of stigma: exploring the health care experiences of kink-oriented patients. *The Journal of Sexual Medicine*, 13(12), 1918–1929. doi: 10.1016/j.jsxm.2016.09.019.

Williams, D. J. & Sprott, R. A. (2022). Current biopsychosocial science on understanding kink. *Current Opinion in Psychology*, 48, 101473. doi: 10.1016/j.copsyc.2022.101473.

Wismeijer, A. A. & van Assen, M. A. (2013). Psychological characteristics of BDSM practitioners. *The Journal of Sexual Medicine*, 10(8), 1943–1952. doi: 10.1111/jsm.12192.

Wright, S. (2006). Discrimination of sm-identifying individuals. *Journal of Homosexuality*, 50, 217-231.

Zimmer, F. & Imhoff, R. (2020). Abstinence from masturbation and hypersexuality. *Archives of Sexual Behavior*, 49(4), 1333–1343. doi: 10.1007/s10508-019-01623-8.

Zwickl, S., Wong, A. F. Q., Dowers, E., Leemaqz, S. Y. L., Bretherton, I., Cook, T., & Cheung, A. S. (2021). Factors associated with suicide attempts among Australian transgender adults. *BMC Psychiatry*, 21(1), 1-9.

Chapter Five

Exploring Erotic Desire

*In his hands I saw a long golden spear and at the end of the
iron tip I seemed to see a point of fire. With this he seemed to
pierce my heart several times so that it penetrated to my entrails.
When he drew it out, I thought he was drawing them out with
it and he left me completely afire with a great love for God. The
pain was so sharp that it made me utter several moans; and so
excessive was the sweetness caused me by this intense pain that
one can never wish to lose it, nor will one's soul be content with
anything less than God. It is not bodily pain, but spiritual,
though the body has a share in it—indeed, a great share. So
sweet are the colloquies of love which pass between the soul and
God that if anyone thinks that I am lying I beseech God, in his
goodness, to give him the same experience.*

Teresa of Avila

What is it that resides on the other side of purity culture? In
the space where we have begun to heal and to ponder what a
new experience of sexuality could entail, we find eroticism.
Within eroticism, we find freedom to form something new for ourselves.
There is room to explore how sexuality and spirituality are intertwined
and provide the soil needed to allow desire to grow and bloom. Eroticism
requires attunement to desire, and desire is an expression of free will. We
choose what it is that we want in the same way that we have a choice in
determining what we want with God. Both need to be chosen and also lead
to revelation about who we are and that for which we long. Longing is a

spiritual practice, and it reveals the deep desires we have for connection, re-connection, and inter-connection with ourselves, with others, and with God. Longing is found both in the pull to return to a pew or to sink your teeth into something you've been warned is forbidden. With this in mind, I invite you to consider where and how eroticism reveals herself and what it may mean for you to embrace a sense of holy eroticism.

Eroticism

As we move into exploring what eroticism is, take a moment to close your eyes and experience several slow breaths. Try to inhabit your own body and to search for the part of you that allows for eroticism and ask it what it means to you. Do you connect it to a spirituality of longing and holy desire? How does it take up space in your life? Is it something you feel connected to, or does it feel intangible to grasp? Perhaps it is something that overwhelms and thus becomes an avoided part of you.

I find that even the word eroticism tends to create a reaction in individuals. I've begun to believe that many people simply view this word as a stand-in for "sexy," and because of things such as purity culture or even personal anxiety, we will simply avoid it. To be honest, history hasn't helped us to embrace eroticism, which is seen, for example, in the Merriam-Webster definition of eroticism: 1) an erotic theme or quality, 2) a state of sexual arousal, and 3) insistent sexual impulse or desire. For a concept with so much life and depth to it, we truly made the word boring. The blandness with which we define eroticism turns us away, continuing a cycle of being forgotten. To the point that many people don't have this concept as part of their vocabulary, let alone their existence.

So, consider this your time to begin to explore how you want to denote eroticism in your own life. There are a few ways to consider the concept of eroticism, one of my favorites comes from Esther Perel, a psychotherapist whose work focuses on human connections and erotic intelligence. Her work gives me hope as she writes that eroticism is "the unexpected yet welcomed touch on a great first date; running into a dear old friend and absconding together for a drink; traveling to a brand new place and experiencing it unfold before you...Eroticism is cultivating pleasure for its own sake. It's about bringing adventure back into play and creativity into our lives" (2023). Dr. Perel and others mention that eroticism is an art, and like art, one's creativity expands the more attention it is given and as it is practiced.

Art is something seen in the day-to-day if we have eyes for it. Eroticism also exists in the day-to-day. This enigma that we often move away from already lives within and around us if we tune into where it might be. Eroticism has something magical and mystical about it, and the allure of this mystery is that it is also part of the mundane. Most of us long for something tangible we can reach out and grab to soothe the anxious mind. Eroticism can be both tangible, and at the same time, it can be the bijou, soul-stirring, sensual thing that we see in a new light or in a new way for the first time. When we expand our definitions of eroticism beyond just genital sex, we begin to take note that it is a typical and normalized part of human existence. We can begin to find it in our thoughts, yearnings, dreams, and hidden impulses when we learn to lower our conditioned filter and open ourselves.

Many of us were taught that to have longings or yearnings might be the things that lead us towards selfishness. Or, that we need to quiet our longings so that we may hear how we are being directed by God. However, it is perhaps more accurate to say that our nature *to long for* begins at the first breath we take as we are crying for touch, warmth, and sustenance. We were designed for longing, and as is evidenced in the quote at the beginning of this chapter by Christian mystic Teresa of Avila, one centuries-old spiritual practice is the embrace of our longings and our erotic desires (of and for the holy). We can all look back to childhood and identify a need that we had that was not met. I say this knowing that all of us come from imperfect places and families. From these unmet needs in childhood our erotic longings in adulthood are formed. Eroticism in adulthood is given life as it is often rooted in early experiences of touch, play, and, at times, even pain. These roots end up being the anchor of our erotic life and point towards the fact that eroticism is something that is building within us, regardless of whether we take note of it or not. This leads one to consider that eroticism was meant to be a part of every being and that to continue in avoidance of this concept can be detrimental to the human condition.

Now is the time to see the goodness that comes from cultivating a relationship with eroticism. This goodness invites us into a space where our minds can slow, and we are invited into creativity. We become more enlivened to what is pulsing around us, calling us to attune to the eroticism already existing in our world. As eroticism begins to unfold within and around us, the goodness of it reminds us that we are all artists. That we look at the blank canvas of our existence and search for a palette that speaks to our dramatic, subtle, lithe, or sensual parts. We begin to use strokes that convey our personal embodiment, zest, aliveness, or sexuality, which are the true antidotes to the death of this world. Eroticism is given life by our creativity. It can be felt and held, yes, between our legs, but also in our minds, our breath, even in the way we stop to notice how the sun warms our skin as it breaks through the bleakness of a cloudy day. The erotic lives in everything. This is the goodness of it – that there is no right or wrong with eroticism, just the freedom to look and find it in the exact space we need it to be.

To add another view of the goodness of eroticism is that it is something we are created to want. We were born with an appetite. We want food. We want sex. We want connection and touch, and yet, we often don't give our appetites attention. For some, there may be the active shutting down of appetite in one area. Ignoring or shutting off parts of ourselves happens when we are deeply wounded or when we don't want to risk opening to another potential harm again. There might be the belief that one has to earn the right to be sensual or sexy or that there is no way a body transformed by time or illness or stress is wanted by another. These falsehoods keep us from our appetites, but our minds and bodies have many touch points that we can't shut down because shutting down appetite in one area impacts all others. Eroticism can be the thing that enlivens us and allows our hunger cues to become present again rather than numbing the ravenous parts of our identity. From this goodness, we begin to see what we gain within our lives as we shift towards embracing what is erotic. What is often a halting place for folks in this journey is identifying how to invite the erotic into one's life.

One of the first, and most challenging, steps is to notice what in our life gives us more energy and, then, to invite more of that thing to be present. The difficulty that lies in this invitation is being able to give yourself permission to slow down, to recognize a want and to risk having that want go ignored if you ask for it and there is no response. But the risk is worth it because we must be present with our being to know what it is we want or what turns us on. So, maybe start with curiosity by completing this sentence. *I know I turn myself on when* _____. We must tune into our bodies to respond to this. A turn-on could be related to sexuality, or it could be about the energy you begin to notice as you connect with yourself at different levels (emotional, spiritual, sexual). Quite literally we can turn ourselves on when we engage with what gives us energy as this means we are tuned into our wants and are connected to our needs, even if there is not a specific goal and we are just responding to our longings in the moment.

Beyond noticing the things in life that bring energy to our soul, we invite the erotic by being emotionally connected to our daily experiences. This means attending to the small moments where we might typically shut down authentic responsiveness in favor of "getting the job done." Take, for instance, eating. This is something we need to be doing about six times a day. It can begin to feel tedious. Or we tell ourselves we are too busy or even that we don't need or deserve sustenance. When we do it, it can be mechanical, or with the air of "I guess I'll just eat whatever is in the fridge" without thinking about what we want or sounds appealing. I understand this approach is something that many of us do without even noticing, so I want to share the raisin exercise with you, which I did not invent but have used in therapy. It is a mindfulness practice to draw our appetites back to the present.

You will need a single raisin for this exercise, and you begin by **holding** the raisin. Place it in your palm or between your finger and thumb. Study it like it's the first time you've ever seen an object like this before in your life. Then, practice **seeing** the raisin, taking time to really focus on it. Gaze on it with care and your entire attention. Let your eyes roam over every crevice and hollow, fold and ridge, and any uniqueness you notice. Next, begin to turn the raisin over between your fingers, **touching** it and exploring the texture. You can even close your eyes if this helps to enhance your sense of touch. Now, lightly hold the raisin under your nose, **smelling** with each breath you take in. Is there any smell, aroma, or fragrance? As you do this, pay attention to anything that may be happening in your mouth or your stomach. Slowly, slowly, bring the raisin up to your lips, noticing how your hand and arm work together, **placing** it exactly where it needs to be. Gently place the raisin in your mouth. Don't chew it but notice how your mouth reacts. Begin to focus on the sensation of the small weight in your mouth, exploring it with your tongue. Perhaps you salivate or perhaps you notice the tension occurring between the excitation and inhibition of this thing you cannot bite into. When you are ready, prepare to chew the raisin, noticing how and where it needs to be in your mouth in order to chew it. Very consciously, take a bite or two, and notice the aftermath. What occurs with the **tasting** of this thing? Are there waves of taste? Without swallowing, tune into the bare sensations of taste and texture in your mouth and if these are changing moment by moment. Begin to notice when the urge for **swallowing** occurs and enjoy this moment you have been waiting for. And finally, try **following** what is left of the raisin as it moves down your throat and into the stomach.

This exercise can tell us quite a bit about ourselves and where we may need more intention – whether it be slowing down, being present, using our senses with daily tasks, or learning how sweet anticipation can be. When we invite eroticism into our lives, we learn to become more mindful of intimate connections. Sometimes this may look like sexual connection while other times it may look like the deepening of connection with a best friend. Learning to tune into curiosity around what conversations or touch brought you energy, what led you to feel revived, or even just doing something new, invites the imagination to take hold. It is with our imagination that sexuality can be transformed, and relationships can be deepened. Our imagination helps us to begin to build the plots for our erotic encounters. The imagination that is part of eroticism keeps our senses vibrant and leads to newness.

Inviting eroticism can also impact play and is often a core component of meaningful connections in life. Play can be both sexual and non-sexual and is a space where creativity can be fed. Play is something that we often forget how to do. As children, we learn how to make believe, how to let ourselves be swept up in stories, and how to turn everyday items into treasures. Along the way, we often lose this most tender part of ourselves. Let us remember that play is crucial for children for development, learning prosocial behavior, and in building a sense of self. It is also just as important in adulthood. In play as an adult, we are using imagination and incredible amounts of boldness and vulnerability. In return, we have the opportunity to know pleasure, connection, or fantasy. When we notice boredom in our sexuality, this can be a signal that it is a good time to be playful with identifying the fantasies and desires that may be missing from a sexual connection. Eroticism leads us to reflect on what touch is most meaningful, what type of play we enjoy with a partner or alone as we signal to our bodies we want pleasure, or even beckons us to engage in something completely new that might bring us great joy.

We can also begin to build a larger capacity for eroticism with a partner(s), which can be incredibly meaningful and bring life back to the spaces that feel dead. When we think about how imagination, creativity, yearning, and being present focused come together, eroticism is often the antidote many of us didn't know we needed. We can build this part of our life by being aware of the small moments (what we enjoyed with a partner that day) and by looking for connecting points, such as the small touch of a lower back as you moved past your partner in the kitchen, the space in a conversation where you felt completely seen, the small breaths you took while you rested your head on your partner's shoulder and noticed how you finally felt settled. These moments build a capacity for the erotic in our lives.

So, I encourage you to give yourself permission to explore the pleasure of life. Invite eroticism into your daily rhythms. Engage it with all your senses. Touch yourself, inhale the scent of skin, taste the sweetness of another, listen for the sounds of pleasure, and look at your own body. Not just as a thing but as a vessel that both gives and receives.

Eroticism is fluid. Like water it can fall from the sky and be dug out of a well. It can form boulders or carve into mountains, and it can be the soft trickle of a summer rain. Eroticism is transformative. It is made in the small moments with the same veracity as in the monumental moments. I find similar meanings in spirituality. Water has a significant place in Holy Scriptures. Christ states, "If you drink from me, you will never thirst again." We see baptism as a major theme in Scripture – being made new and being cherished as a result of water. Or, when Christ was crucified, we are told both blood and water flowed out of his dying body. Is there a space for eroticism and the spiritual to mingle and become something new?

Holy Eroticism

We are yearning for something new. Purity culture was able to twist something that was intended for good and to warp it into a tool for shame and disconnection. Purity culture taught us that there wasn't a place for God in our authentic sexuality. It mangled the view we held of our bodies, worth, and longing. We were pushed into the shadows and convinced that we did not deserve to be seen. And, yet, there is a glimmer within many of us that things were supposed to be different. That what we learned is no longer acceptable, healthy, or holy. That we were meant for a deeper connection. We were meant for holy eroticism.

Holy eroticism is powerful. One of the strongest and most sacred forces that propels us forward, beyond our own existence and into communion with another and with God. It can look a thousand different ways and mean different things to different people. This type of eroticism is fluid in that it can take shape and form as needed for each person searching for it. It can live in the depth of us and devours the body and the soul and from it comes the power and the knowledge that all is within reach. Every desire, every longing, every hunger can be fulfilled.

Holy eroticism can show up similarly to a "still small voice" by drawing the eye to a flush, the shift in the space between, the small movements of a throat swallowing. It can offer us an acute attunement to our bodies so that we feel each sensation our skin encounters and turn it into our most prized possession. Like a sense of spirituality, holy eroticism can be found anywhere when we have "eyes to see and ears to hear." Holy eroticism, at its fullest, draws energy out of us to fulfill desires of others as well. We need this type of eroticism to move beyond ourselves to greater love and care for "the least of these," our neighbor, our world, and for God. Holy eroticism is the internal pull that tugs at us and says, "There is something deeper for you." It leads us towards something bigger than ourselves.

Holy eroticism can entail looking with eyes of both faith and desire to see that we were called into the erotic by the Creator. It can help us see that we can find communion with God in the small moments of life, moments that cause us to be still and to notice the extraordinary in the unremarkable movements of a day. The erotic can lead us into moments when we sense an eagerness to know more or when we've seen something in a different light for the first time. Holy eroticism is what we notice when we engage all our senses in a moment of worship, and we tune into the rhythms of a service – clasping hands, standing, praying, smelling the incense, the taste of Holy Eucharist as it lingers on our tongues. Our energy can come from the connection with the sacred.

We might fall on our knees for a lover much like we would in prayer because the Holy that surrounds us in both instances can frighten, even though we cannot look away. We are so enamored and drawn towards something more that we cannot help but be moved by this thing that feels other worldly. It reminds me of a Leonard Cohen lyric in his song, "I'm Your Man," as he sings, "I'd crawl to you baby and I'd fall at your feet. And I'd howl at your beauty like a dog in heat." We can do nothing but pant because we are starved for more, and perhaps our longing can lead us to the thing or the One who can satisfy our hunger and quench our thirst.

Or perhaps holy eroticism could be seen as a way in which God calls us out of separation and into (re)union. Sexuality and eroticism are both incredible forces in our lives. They can be the source of joy, yearning, anxiety, shame, and curiosity. They can also be forces by which we recognize a hunger for connection and harmony with God. When we stop to look deep enough, we might find that buried in our conscious pursuit of sex is an unconscious pursuit of God. That is, in the same way we might ask a lover, we are often also asking God, "Do you love me? Do you care about me? Do you want me? Am I important to you? Am I good enough?" No matter how holy eroticism presents itself there is room to see the goodness of it and to see that it comes from God as a reflection of the original design for humankind, which is to be surrounded by creation in communion with a Creator.

Out of holy eroticism comes holy work. The cries of the earth and the Creator calling us to move beyond ourselves to construct a world where there is both equity and equality is holy eroticism. Holy work fueled by our calling and desire for communion in all aspects of our existence means that we do not turn away but stand and bear witness to the travesties that so many have endured, such as racism, homophobia, sexism, classism, genocide. These are things we need to acknowledge, apologize for, and then, offer reparations. This is what it means to bring all things into a union that is holy.

When holy eroticism is at play, we are truly able to embody the greatest commandment to love God, and from that love, we love others. The holy work of social justice is one of the best ways to evince this commandment because it focuses on aligning with those who are oppressed and maligned by society. We have many souls to look at and see what holy work looks like – Dr. Martin Luther King Jr., Mother Teresa, Nelson Mandela, Rebiya Kadeer, Shirin Ebadi – and this list could cover pages. We, too, can join the endeavor of selfless work that seeks to benefit others and is guided by the call to do the hard and holy work of loving our neighbors.

When we let holy eroticism guide us, we learn to elevate the personhood of Jesus by leaning into social justice, and we do this knowing it manifests holy love. It reminds us that every being is created in the divine image of God, even when it doesn't fit our script of people. We see the divine image in persons who are refugees, immigrants, poor, neurodivergent, criminals, queer, or different in any way from yourself. While we are surrounded by systems of political and religious groups that often end up dehumanizing others, our participation in holy work makes sure we never forget that we are part of divine humanity and that all people are made to be in connection with one another and their God. Social justice, maybe more than any other task set forth in religious teachings, implores us always to see the divine image of God in every person. When we enter the work of social justice, invited by our holy eroticism, it is then that our souls and our minds can be touched by the injustice that divides us before we are moved towards the holy work of reunification.

When we are engaged in the holy work that can be born from our own eroticism, we fight for the human dignity of others. We seek to change the systems that perpetuate the inequalities that divide humankind. We look out for those who cannot look out for themselves. We march, and we protest. This is living in holy eroticism. This is the holy work that heals division and fosters connectedness.

An Invitation to Holy Eroticism

Sexuality and spirituality spring from the same vital life source and have the same end. They are both about relationship; loving and being loved; desiring and being desired; and being vulnerable, honest, and intimate. They both require growth in self-knowledge, including awareness of one's limitations and "shadow." They both involve the whole self, including body and emotions...These are not two different forces, nor are they in any way at odds with each other. (Giblin, 2014, p. 79)

Spiritual practice can be defined in many ways, but one way that I think of it is as anything that unfolds our attention to the existence and presence of God with us. Historically, this comes in the form of prayer, scripture reading, worshiping through song, and even attending church. But culture always shifts, and there is more openness regarding approaches to spiritual practice. For example, we now consider things such as watching a sunrise, caring for others, and discovering new scientific verities to be spiritual. Divine presence is found anywhere, much like we are shown in Psalm 139:7-12. Here, we see that God is in everything and found everywhere. As Paul reminds us later, God is in and through all things, and by knowing that, we can find holiness in any space. Let us consider holy eroticism as a spiritual practice.

As humans created for holy eroticism, we crave transcendence, either consciously or unconsciously. How does sex get us to that state, and what can happen there? How does spirituality get us to a space where we move beyond ourselves? Where we get to feel free and get out of our heads so we might discover a new openness where there is room for joy and space and we let go and give up control? How does spirituality get us to a place where we might be elevated into something unknown? This is where we can move towards inviting holy eroticism into our everyday life. In the book, *Tantric Jesus: The Erotic Heart of Early Christianity,* the author writes, "Eros (or what we could think of as holy eroticism) drives us to seek union with the sacred. It leads us to find love and ecstasy and presence in all aspects of our world...The erotic life is our life of deep desire, including our instinctual cravings for food and water, our sexual longings, our drive to create beauty and art, and our refined compassionate desires to serve the good of others and the planet. This erotic life is both highly spiritual and deeply physical" (p. 14). The author mentions "deep desire," and this is what drives us towards what is sacred and what is physical. This helps us to recognize that we are given a desire for more than what purity culture tells us we can have.

What is meaningful about an erotically sexual practice (as a spiritual practice) is that it helps us to step outside of our rational minds. No longer are we bogged down by the day's stress. We stop with the demands, the guilt, and the strife of life that weighs heavy. Much like the peace that can be felt and the change in consciousness that can happen during contemplation or prayer, eroticism – sexual or not – can help with a "regression" of the focus on trivial parts of life and move us into the spaces where our values rest. By taking these mental breaks, we are reinvigorating the body and becoming more open to a new sense of wonder. We are turning on new parts of our brain and spirit to create something new, quite like a "born again" experience.

As people, we are constantly becoming. We create or recreate ourselves across the lifespan. The birth of a new "self" requires us to shift beliefs, desires, and freedoms to bring about the new self, and this requires an openness to a new balance. Often, we experience an inner shift in our balance through eroticism, and the new balance actually has to do with spiritual practice. Yet, the greatest impediment to spiritual practice and growth is us. We might long for our souls to soar, but our human mind often prevents an experience like this. We struggle to be open-minded or to stare in awe. We catastrophize about new experiences, and we only focus on personal wellbeing. We lose the chance for growth by being in a stance of defensiveness, which is always a posture of aggressive energy towards ourselves and towards others.

Part of the reason I love being a psychologist is that I get to be alongside humans as they persevere to move through the parts of themselves that limit the growth of a new self. I've been able to witness the moments when a person senses a pull within themself, a pull that says "grow, move, want" and also wrestles with the parts of an old self that say, "It's safest to remain stagnant." Humans can do deep work, making peace between what is fearful and what is freeing. This is often the case when it comes to a new spiritual self, when we lean into the new practices that begin to move us towards freedom. When our human spirit becomes whole, the new self fits, and finally, we are transformed into the "self" we were created to become.

Holy eroticism creates a break in the familiar, which allows us to loosen control and to let the spirit lead. I realize that religion often promises these experiences with a mission trip, church camp, or a church retreat – where we leave the "normal" behind. Yet, deep spiritual practice is the act of release in which we free our erotic spirit that is already ever present and a part of our being. Like acts of prayer and meditation, eroticism can move us into creative spaces and foster transformation of the self. This transformation is a type of healing that God provides as part of spiritual maturation so we might become fully integrated and fully free. Integration allows us to keep from aggressively strong-arming certain parts of ourselves, leading us to internally shut down the parts we have that are deemed "bad" or "wild."

Instead of waiting for these parts to break open, we use the path to these parts as growth. Instead of "praying away" the parts we think we need to cut off, we turn inward and seek to unearth what lurks beneath the surface, yearning to be free. Instead of trying to eliminate sexual parts of ourselves through denial, control, and restraint, we embrace that God created sexual diversity and that this diversity enriches the spirit. We don't need to escape ourselves. There is no war between "flesh" and "spirit." There is only a body full of breath, awe, honesty, gratitude, and goodwill. Our eroticism and sexuality lead us to an embodied way of existing – as female and male, differing gender expressions, our sundry orientations, our desire for sensuous touch in this world, and our hunger for life. Genitally active or celibate, single or partnered, young or aged, disabled or able-bodied, by the goodness of God we are made to be sexual beings from birth to death (Nelson, 2006).

Much of holy eroticism requires a person to be connected to their body. Not surprisingly, alienation of the self by splitting between flesh and spirit fractures our ability to engage in genuine erotic pleasure and holistic intimacy with the self, God, and others. We cannot view the body as the enemy because this fixation causes us to forget our existence as embodied humans is designed to mirror God's goodness and love for all people.

Embodiment is much needed in a process of holy eroticism. Positive embodiment is associated with a sanctified view of one's body where it is assumed that the body is holy, worthy of respect, and integral to one's being (Jacobson et al., 2016).

Let us not forget that the core of eroticism is love. It is a love for life, for creation, for self, and for others. I invite you to embrace that you possess the capacity to love much more than you think you do. Do not give life to the rational and self-conscious parts of yourself to trick you out of the hard and holy work of finding true and passionate eroticism. Our passion is shaped by God's passion. Therefore, we don't need to fear our sexuality, and we don't need to fear God. Eroticism doesn't have to be a place where we diverge from our spirituality. Rather, it can be a place where we learn to see that eroticism is integral to a deep and lasting desire for the Divine. You are a sexual being. Your body guides you to connect with others and with God. Your sexuality and your eroticism is the embodiment of the longing you possess for perfect union. Your desire and longing beckon you too be known and to know others, to give voice to your desire through the language of skin and spirit.

Get Curious

1. What part of your past informs your experience of eroticism?

2. Complete the raisin exercise a few times in the upcoming days and be mindful about what you begin to notice.

3. What is erotic for you?

4. How do you want to practice holy eroticism?

Chapter Five References

"Eroticism." *Merriam-Webster Dictionary*. Retrieved on October 28, 2023 from https://www.merriam-webster.com/dictionary/eroticism.

Giblin, P. (2014). Men reconnecting spirituality and sexuality. *Journal of Spirituality in Mental Health*, 16(2), 74-88.

Jacobson, H. L., Hall, M. E. L., Anderson, T. L., & Willingham, M. M. (2016). Religious beliefs and experiences of the body: an extension of the developmental theory of embodiment. *Mental Health, Religion & Culture*, 19(1), 52-67. doi: 10.1080/13674676.2015.1115473.

Nelson, J. (2006). Embracing the erotic: the church's unfinished sexual revolution. *Yale Divinity School*. Retrieved on October 31, 2023 from https://reflections.yale.edu/article/sex-and-church/embracing-erotic-church-s-unfinished-sexual-revolution.

Peers, E. A. (1991). *The life of Teresa of Jesus: An autobiography of Teresa of Avila*. Image Books, pp 192 -193.

Perel, E. (2023). *Focus on: Eroticism*. Retrieved October 28, 2023, from https://www.estherperel.com/focus-on-categories/eroticism.

Reho, J. H. (2017). *Tantric Jesus: The erotic heart of early Christianity*. Destiny Books.

Chapter Six

Liberating Pleasure

Passion is an energy, a drive from within. The French call it elan vital, a creative force. It's a thirst for union, a thirst for myself, for more of true life. As such, passion surprisingly carries with it some inevitable dissatisfaction. It never lasts and is never enough once you feed on it. Passion constantly creates within you a hole that longs to be filled. In the Christian tradition we call such implanted longing the indwelling Holy Spirit. The Spirit keeps yearning in us for union with more—with ourselves and thus with God.

Richard Rohr

A s you enter this final chapter of the book, I hope there is a recognition that some of the baggage that purity culture told you was yours to hold is no longer feeling as heavy. I hope there is a lightness about you that you didn't know was possible. I hope there is the desire to confront the perfidious sexual stereotypes and expectations with new and more accurate information. I hope there is a desire to embrace more elements of sex and intimacy as you are now more prepared to celebrate and take ownership of pleasure. I hope there is less shame and that it continues to decrease as you find you can share your own story more and more. I invite you, now, to begin to envision a future where you lean into sexual empowerment by considering the question, "What story do you want to write that will honor the beautiful, unique gift that is the sensual, powerful you?" (Sellers, 2017, p. 111).

Pleasure

Pleasure is part of the human experience as much as suffering is, and as humans, we seem resigned to the fact that we will suffer. In fact, after moving through a tumultuous season of life, we say that we were changed (usually for the better) by the suffering we had endured. It is interesting that we are so accepting of suffering, but often, we cannot find it within ourselves to believe that we also deserve pleasure. It seems that the church forgot that pleasure holds just as much meaning, if not more, than suffering.

One of the first places we could look to see the concept of pleasure and suffering is in The Passion story. When we consider the crucifixion of Christ, we see how there was immense suffering (the word passion comes from the Latin word for suffering, *patiens*) in the brutal death that occurred. But the thrust of the story is the pleasure that unfolds because of such suffering. The death of Christ leads to the evisceration of hell and eternal death being defeated. Beyond this, the fulfillment of scripture, prophesy, and the purpose of Jesus was fulfilled. From this fulfillment, we are given true life. We are invited into an existence where we can experience pleasure. However, purity culture did something to our relationship with pleasure, which led to a fear that many people hold regarding the concept of pleasure. Many of us are still stuck in a place where pleasure is too much of a sexy word or it frightens us, so we avoid it. Or we think of pleasure as sinful in some way (greedy or selfish). Many of us spent years in spaces where religious culture promoted the idea that pleasure took us further *away from* God rather than *closer to* God.

As a therapist, I often see people because of a lack of pleasure. Not just in a sexual way, but in other ways. For example, a person will cut themselves off from pleasure, such as those suffering from disordered eating. When I work with these individuals with this concern, I often ask what role pleasure or desire plays in their life or their recovery from disordered eating. Almost all of them endorse a life that is absent of both. No pleasure in food, community, or sex. Desire is something they are actively erasing from their lives to sustain an eating disorder. During the recovery process, people tend to reconnect with pleasure in their life. It is beautiful to see this happen, and it is often a sign that a person is moving closer to a true self and further from disordered eating. There are many markers of this, but behaviorally, I see more freedom to eat, to rest, and to pay attention to and nurture both body and spirit.

A person who has pleasure has purpose, but one of the most difficult parts of accepting pleasure is that most people think it is something to be earned – much like the mentality that says, "If I work out all week, I can have a cheat day on Saturday." Yet, pleasure isn't something to be earned. There is no proving that you deserve pleasure. Within and outside of sexuality, we all have the right to pleasure. We are allowed to feel good and to have not done a single thing to earn that. It is not selfish to want pleasure, but even if it was, so what? In a safe and consensual sexual space, maybe it's ok to take what you want. You are allowed to ask for "more" or "softer" or to state, "Don't stop."

Pleasure is not something to be earned, and it is not something to be ignored. Do not give in to the purity culture belief that your body is to be used and discarded. Do not submit. Do not lay down quietly, but instead, with a voice of power, claim what it is your body longs for. Wonder what your soul is longing for, and open yourself to touch that is different, touch that beckons us to risk a new experience, learning a new way to inhabit the skin that you can't stop touching and learning. At times, sexuality can feel tiresome or uninspiring. You could keep muddling through, but it may be that doing so distances you from pleasure. Do you have to continue this way? Or is there a risk that you feel willing to take in order to follow the desire that is calling to you?

There is goodness in the desire moving you towards pleasure. We were made for pleasure, and again, let's remember the thousands of pleasure receptors in the clitoris. Let us also remember the fact that we have a "pleasure center" in our brains. Humans code pleasure in the orbitofrontal cortex – a space in the brain where this processing has taken place since the creation of humans. This is another way that we are shown that pleasure is from the Divine. It is an inherently created part of who we are, and we are hardwired for it.

We also see goodness in pleasure when we tune in to the fact that pleasure is about what you do in your life to nurture your spirit and your liveliness. In life, we typically begin to feel competent and like we've achieved something when we sense mastery or when we take notice of the intrinsic reward that comes from doing things that benefit others. While these are a good and natural part of life, pleasure is more related to how you engage with these processes, more so than the activity with which you are engaged. Pleasure is alive when we can be fully present and fully experience whatever process we are immersed within, and much like we might find the Holy Spirit present in everything, we can also be open to seeing that pleasure can always be found because it comes from within us.

On the other side of purity culture we find pleasure. We learn that sexuality is not about purity or sin or true love waiting. It is bigger than that. It is access to another world, another space where we don't have to be contained, and we do not have to do anything but tune into the rhythms within your own being. It is only when we find our own pleasure, when we finally acknowledge the longing that we live with, that we can begin to advocate for those around us. To stop doing and start being by beginning to fight for others to find the erotic within their own life. As we expand our belief and acceptance that we have the right to pleasure, I think we can change things. If we are content with pursuing pleasure, maybe we could stop engaging in the things that hurt communities, people groups, and our earth.

Pleasure Activism

The invitation is to fight for your pleasure. The right to sexual pleasure is more intricate than just stating what you want during a sexual encounter. It involves raising up women and reframing conversations about human rights. Capitalism and patriarchy built a web that entraps our pleasure and holds it hostage. The sexuality and rights to pleasure of many peoples are dictated and oppressed by those who are terrified of you finding power within the pleasure you could experience.

Truly, there is power in our pleasure. Audre Lorde, a self-described "black, lesbian, mother, warrior, poet," wrote an essay (among many other amazing works) in which she stated that by accessing erotic knowledge, which I would say is needed for pleasure, we disrupt the oppressed feelings we hold and begin to evaluate our existence. We may begin to ask, *"Who am I? What am I? How am I settling in life? What am I ignoring? What am I letting control me?"* Asking these questions disrupts the systems that keep us quiet, tired, and producing through the work of our bodies. Lorde (1984) noted, "Recognizing the power of the erotic within our lives can give us the energy to pursue genuine change in our world, rather than merely settling for a shift of characters in the same weary drama. For not only do we touch our most profoundly creative source, but we do that which is female and self-affirming in the face of a racist, patriarchal, and anti-erotic society" (p. 59).

If you were to center pleasure in your life – sexual, spiritual, relational – and believe that it was truly meant for you, how would your world be different? When you acknowledge that pleasure holds space in your life, and you integrate this into your views and values, you will begin to see how you and those around you have the right to a good, pleasurable life. This realization has the potential to see others in a new way as you consider that they, too, have the right to a good, pleasurable life. This is especially important as we consider that many who hold marginalized identities are actively still politically fighting for the right to gain their own power and claim pleasure.

Those who inhabit marginalized bodies are well aware of the connection between power and pleasure. If you, like me, are inhabiting a body with privileged identities, then it may be news to know that there already exists a long and extensive Black feminist erotic philosophy. My privilege often hides knowledge like this from me. One modern educator of pleasure is adrienne maree brown who discusses the idea of pleasure activism in her book, *Pleasure Activism: The Politics of Feeling Good* (2019). She states, "Pleasure activism is the work we do to reclaim our whole, happy, and satisfiable selves from the impacts, delusions, and limitations of oppression and/or supremacy." She goes on to say, "Pleasure—embodied, connected pleasure—is one of the ways we know when we are free. That we are always free. That we always have the power to co-create the world. Pleasure helps us move through the times that are unfair, through grief and loneliness, through the terror of genocide, or days when the demands are just overwhelming. Pleasure heals the places where our hearts and spirit get wounded. Pleasure reminds us that even in the dark, we are alive. Pleasure is a medicine for the suffering that is absolutely promised in life" (437-438).

I would imagine the question coming up for you is, "*Okay, so how do I 'do' pleasure activism?*" We always want to figure out how to "do" instead of how to "be," but before we move to "doing," maybe we can begin with a very simple self-inquiry by wondering about what feels right to you. This helps us to see our own story and eroticism as the map for understanding. By asking a simple question, what we are doing is turning in towards ourselves for wisdom rather than looking to external influences and authorities to tell us what we desire. This is the start of reclaiming pleasure as power as it moves one to dismiss the idea that others know more about us than we do, and we begin to learn that we do not have to experience this life and our body in prescribed ways.

Pleasure activism also centers making justice and liberation one of the most pleasurable experiences we can have. Purity culture told us our bodies were not our own, that they belonged to another. We engage in pleasure activism when we release ourselves from the false messages of purity and reclaim ourselves as beings. This is the liberating work of embodying who we really are. Purity culture tells us that pleasure is something that not everyone has access to (although we know most privileged identities – particularly white and male – have held this access out of reach), but pleasure activism helps us to reclaim our full selves by taking back our access to pleasure.

Claiming access to the human right for pleasure means we look at all bodies – white, brown, able-bodied, trans – with wonder and awe. We see each person as a being with the right to pleasure. For many folks, the messaging for centuries says that our miraculous flesh is inferior, marred in some way, or is meant to be fetishized. So, push back against this. Take yourself in. Look at your own nakedness. Explore pleasure. See yourself as belonging to you and to no one else. Then, look around you and see where pleasure needs to be nourished and distributed to those in your world.

If you are someone who is not experiencing pleasure or struggles to recall your last experience of pleasure, then this is the time to allow yourself to want for more. Not just for yourself, but for those who came before you and fought for the freedom to have pleasure and beat down the doors of those who withheld it. It is time to want more for yourself. By doing so, you are also carving a path for those who come after you to know that their pleasure can be claimed. When you have access to pleasure, you can be a fuller version of yourself, and you will find you are capable of more than you ever dared hope.

Sexuality and Empowerment

When we believe we have the right to pleasure and seize what was intended for us in this life, we notice the empowered way we might live. We become confident in all aspects of our identity, especially as who we are as sexual beings. We notice confidence in the fact that we all have sexual rights, that we can possess bodily autonomy, and that we engage in consensual sexual experiences informed by the pleasure you and desire. We embrace the exploration of your interests and curiosities without fear and shame, and our empowerment leads us to liberation.

For so long we were told what our (women's) pleasure was and who it was for. Even the female orgasm is commandeered by men's sexuality. The female orgasm becomes the pinnacle of the same old song and dance that women are expected to perform as part of heterosexual sex. There are magazines and blogs everywhere telling women how to be the "sexual best" for a partner, and they offer tips about having orgasms, which eventually teach women they must be positioned around men's bodies. They teach women that the female body is a thing to be tamed and, ultimately, controlled. In addition, the female orgasm is often treated as a currency. It's the "next step" for a man to get what he wants in order to achieve an orgasm of his own because, as we "know" (as we are told), sex ends when a male ejaculates.

Some researchers take note that "the orgasm imperative and orgasm gap have constructed an understanding of female pleasure dependent on men's work and skill – creating an obligation for men to 'give' orgasms to women and creating an obligation for women to deliver an orgasm (fake or real) in exchange to reward the man's work and affirm his status as a lover" (2016, p 742-743). Other research concurs that men feel more masculine and have higher sexual esteem when they think women orgasmed during a sexual encounter and that men are disappointed if their female partner doesn't orgasm. In fact, research shows that men are reluctant to have a women orgasm via vibrator because of their own personal inadequacy (Chadwich and van Anders, 2017). To counter this social conditioning, female sexual empowerment looks like naming our pleasure, calling out to it, having non-procreative sex, and real orgasms. Our bodies have been repurposed for other people's motives for so long that it is truly a protest when we find personal pleasure in our orgasms. Empowerment is finding the right tools and knowledge to create a new sexual narrative where our orgasm is not centered on our partners but, instead, on our own pleasure.

Sexual pleasure is a human right and one we can fight for. The World Association for Sexual Health (WAS), in September 2021, ratified a Declaration on Sexual Pleasure in its General Assembly. This was done to urge all who hold influence in society to recognize the vital importance of sexual pleasure as a major component of sexual health and sexual rights. The Global Advisory Board of Sexual Health and Wellbeing (GAB) defines sexual pleasure as the physical and/or psychological satisfaction and enjoyment derived from solitary or shared erotic experiences, including thoughts, dreams and autoeroticism. Self-determination, consent, safety, privacy, confidence and the ability to communicate and negotiate sexual relations are key enabling factors for pleasure to contribute to sexual health and wellbeing.

Sexual pleasure should be exercised within the context of sexual rights, particularly the rights to equality and nondiscrimination, autonomy and bodily integrity, and the right to the highest attainable standard of health and freedom of expression. The experiences of human sexual pleasure are diverse, and sexual rights ensure that pleasure is a positive experience for all concerned and not obtained by violating other people's human rights and wellbeing (GAB, 2016). This exhaustive definition reminds us that sexual pleasure is integral in the recognition of women's political and economic integrity and empowerment. Female sexual pleasure means we have control over our bodies and the right to choose what we do with our bodies. We decide whether we allow or forbid others to be involved with our bodies.

When we choose to be with our own bodies, we are making space for empowerment to occur. Let's remember that western female sexuality (even when we are sexually alone with our bodies) are shaped by so many factors that disempower us. Some even say it is "excessive" (i.e., not necessary for the purposes of reproduction of male pleasure) (McClelland and Fine, 2008). Women are often stuck at being just the "right" amount of sexual, not sexual enough, or sexually excessive. We live with the messages of our role to solicit and appreciate male attention while also being named as the gatekeepers of male sexuality. We need to look nice, but not sexy and not like a slut. We need to act nice, but be flirty and easy, though not a whore and definitely not a prude. All these bullshit ideas about the female body and sexuality leave us exhausted.

Empowerment, therefore, can look like experiencing our sexuality in a way that is excessive. For instance, with solo pleasure, females can experience their sexuality in a way that is non-conforming to the dominant, male messages of sexuality. Women don't have to worry about pregnancy during solo pleasure, and we become the provider of pleasure rather than needing anyone else to be present. We only need to be concerned with our own pleasure. In this way, recognizing that we are entitled to and are able to experience pleasure is an expression of sexual empowerment.

When women are empowered, anything is possible. Empowered women engage in pleasure activism. Empowered women engage in holy work. They impact generations as they both push boundaries and frighten those who have selfishly held power for so long. Empowered women are not afraid of their creativity. Empowered women do not stifle the parts of themselves that long to burst forth and create something new. Empowered women bare their teeth and say, "No more." They protect those they love. They create deep intimate communities with other women, and they search for pleasure in any space they choose.

Erotic Justice and Erotic Capabilities

When we are seeking pleasure and are empowered to find it, we can no longer live as if pleasure is optional. Pleasure exists for me, for you, and for all those who draw breath. Every being is capable of experiencing the erotic, and when we are able to see eroticism as a capability rather than solely a part of pleasure or satisfaction, what we are doing is truly leaning into the transformative power of the erotic (Lorde, 1984). We can take hold of the belief that sex isn't just biological or psychological fulfillment but is a resource that can nourish self-worth and personal discovery. It can deepen connections with others, and in this way, the erotic becomes a vehicle for empowerment and inter-connection. Our view changes to seeing the erotic as a basic human freedom that is needed for a burgeoning life, rather than as a luxury that is only available to few. The empowerment of the erotic leads us to begin thinking about the social and cultural factors that impact a person's ability to grasp pleasure and eroticism. This is particularly important because some suggest that denying a person's erotic potentiality is ostensibly a form of dehumanization, as the denial of a part of someone's personhood (Nussbaum, 1995).

In capability philosophy, Nussbaum (2011) touched on a philosophy she wanted society to consider. Through this she identifies what is known as central capabilities, which include bodily integrity, practical reason, bodily health, control over one's environment, affiliation, senses, imagination, thoughts, and emotions. These capabilities were created to be seen as new or potentially a unified perspective on issues that are typically siloed. Tsui (2022) used Nussbaum's research to explore erotic capabilities that she proposed to help society assess and promote entitlement for erotic choices and freedoms in our everyday lives. Tsui identified erotic capabilities as freedom from sexual coercion or deprivation, democratized sexual knowledge, sexual health options, inclusive spaces for diversified erotic expressions, erotic affiliation and negotiation, and diversified erotic aspirations, fulfillments, and experimentations. Tsui's study helped to shape a view of how sexuality is a vehicle of empowerment that can be cultivated and can illuminate the potential to imagine and create agentic and pleasurable moments for people in all social locations under the patriarchy we still live under.

Every person needs access to erotic capabilities. Each person deserves equitable, enjoyable, and empowering pleasure. When we take note of erotic justice, we begin to learn that a just society accommodates the needs of sexually active people just as readily as it accommodates those who find emotional fulfillment in non-sexual relationships. In an erotically just culture, there is no celebration of specific values or lifestyles. Instead, it finds its purpose in cultivating erotic capabilities so that each person can imagine and express their ideal sexual self. We are in great need of erotic justice. Societally, we need to begin to pay more attention to what pursuing justice in desires looks like for us. We can consider erotic justice and how it "resonates with the values of dignity and equality that surely we all yearn for in those aspects of our lives that are life-affirming—love, care, connection with others... and our general health and well-being" (Van Zyl, 2105, p 148). There should be equal access to the erotic and to desire for each person who is searching for it.

Erotic justice is demonstrated when we can allow our longings to be personally driven rather than prescribed, when we give life to our own preferences and choices regarding our bodies, and when we truly begin to advocate for the sexual wants and needs that we have. Erotic justice comes from sexual self-exploration that draws us closer to ourselves and where we have access to joy, fun, pleasure, tension, release, and empowerment (Van Zyl, 2015; Bowman, 2014). Erotic justice is based on the belief that each person is entitled to dignity and equality regarding their bodies and erotic identities (Jolly et al., 2013: Van Zyl, 2015). This justice becomes inspiring and can spread to other, non-sexual, arenas of life, much like some researchers have noted that empowered women may often "move from negotiations for orgasms to demands for a guarantee to other rights" (Jolly et al, 2013, p 21). When we learn to fight for our pleasure, we become an unstoppable force.

I invite you, now, to become the person you feel like you can't be in other spaces. Find your values. Align your pleasure with your values and become...*more*. I believe each woman is made with a sort of hornet's nest within her body. We are told the nest is delicate, that we shouldn't jostle it, and that we must constantly strive to keep the hornets from buzzing too loud or stinging. But, if the nest is never prodded, then how will we ever know the strength, and the sting, and the fight we have within us?

Purity culture was the lie that kept us docile, kept us giving and giving. It was the lie that told us never to take for ourselves. It said pleasure was only meant for some and at certain times. It told women they were both not enough and too much. It made us strangers in our skin. It crushed the dreams of men and women alike. It was the snake in the grass that always found a way to strike.

Just remember, it is a woman whom we see crushing the head of a snake, dealing death to something that should never have been given life. So, start fighting for your pleasure because pleasure will help us to remember that when this world was made by the Creator, we were designed to live in a lush and beautiful space eating and roaming and being in our naked bodies.

Chapter Six References

Bowman, C. P. (2014). Women's Masturbation: Experiences of sexual empowerment in a primarily sex-positive Sample. *Psychology of Women Quarterly*, 38(3), 363-378. doi: 10.1177/0361684313514855.

brown, adrienne maree (2019). *Pleasure activism: The politics of feeling good*. AK Press.

Jolly, S., Cornwall, A., & Hawkins, K. (Eds.) (2013). *Women, sexuality and the political power of pleasure*. Bloomsbury Publishing.

Lorde, A. (1984). Uses of the erotic: the erotic as power. In *Sister outsider. Freedom*. Crossing Press, pp. 53–59.

McClelland, S. I. & Fine, M. (2008). Rescuing a theory of adolescent sexual excess: Young women and wanting. In A. Harris (Ed.), *Next wave cultures: Feminism, subcultures, activism* (pp. 83–102). Routledge.

Nussbaum, M. C. (1995). Objectification. *Philosophy & Public Affairs*, 24(4), 249-291.

Porter, C. N., Douglas, N, & Collumbien, M. (2017). Enhance pleasure and grip your strength: Men's Health magazine and pseudo-reciprocal pleasure. *Culture, Health, and Sexuality*, 19(7), 738-751.

Rohr, R (2017, November 13). Purity and passion. *Center for Action and Contemplation*. Retrieved November 18, 2023, from https://cac.org/daily-meditations/purity-and-passion-2017-11-13.

Rohr, R. (2019, October 15). Diversity and communion. *Center for Action and Contemplation*. Retrieved October 24, 2023, from https://cac.org/daily-meditations/diversity-and-communion-2019-10-21/.

Sellers, T. S. (2017). *Sex, God, and the Conservative Church* (1st ed.). Taylor and Francis. Retrieved from https://www.perlego.com/book/1517289/sex-god-and-the-conservative-church-erasing-shame-from-sexual-intimacy-pdf.

Van Zyl, M. (2015). Taming monsters: theorizing erotic justice in Africa. *Agenda*, 29(1), 147 -154.

Working definition of sexual pleasure (2016). *Global Advisory Board for Sexual Health and Wellbeing*. Retrieved from http://www.gab-shw.org/our-work/working-defin-ition-of-sexual-pleasure.

Epilogue

Re-Imagining Your Story

This book began by acknowledging the true darkness I lived in for many years of my young life. Purity culture was a cage I was stuck in – a prison, where there were rules, consequences, and what felt like no way out. But the truth I learned is that freedom from purity messages and the shame and enduring pain is possible. There is no way around it and no way to avoid it. I had to go through the process of unlearning so that I could discover how to heal the wounds within myself and to find what resides on the other side of purity culture. On the other side there is justice, the kind Plato described as balance and harmony, but also the kind of justice that won't be silenced until fairness can be felt by all people.

On the other side, I found myself. My true self. I found the me that can make choices on my own, the me who still feels a little lost but seeks union with a God who created me and my body for pleasure and is so much revealing the erotic. I found the me that can build lasting connection, and the me who has the power to reauthor my story, not allowing any other person to try to write it for me.

Where are you, and what will you find on the other side of purity culture?

What will your story be?

It's time for you to begin reimagining your sexuality.

www.ingramcontent.com/pod-product-compliance
Lightning Source LLC
Chambersburg PA
CBHW020352130626
46549CB00006B/2275